# We Were Not Alone

*a Community Building Art Works anthology*

*Edited by:*
*Hari Alluri & Seema Reza*

*Introduction by:*
*Jewel*

**CBAW**

*Community Building Art Works.*

We Were Not Alone: a Community Building Art Works anthology
©2021

published by Community Building Art Works

www.communitybuildingartworks.org

Printed in the United States of America

Cover Art: Joe Merritt
Book & Cover Design: Garrett Bryant


ISBN (print): 978-0-578-30155-6
ISBN (ebook): 978-0-578-31025-1

BOOK EDITORS
Hari Alluri
Seema Reza

SELECTION TEAM
Amelia Bane
Shuly Xóchitl Cawood
Preeti Kaur Dhaliwal
Dartinia Hull
Arthur Kayzakian
Diana Osborn
Martha Pedersen
Erik Schwab
Ben Weakley
Kendra Whitfield
Miden Wood

OUR PAST & CURRENT BOARD MEMBERS—
who build the foundation from which this work grows.
Amelia Bane
Anselm Beech
Amy Bontrager
Bryan Doerries
Akhil Iyer
Amanda Kelly
Colin McKee
Joe Merritt
Christiana Musk
Wytold Lebing
Rina Shah
Kevin Trujillo
Willie Young

# Contents

## We Were Not Alone

## Your Own Gestures and Symbols    41

# Introduction
## by Jewel

When I first met Seema and learned of the work that Community Building Art was doing, my soul leapt with recognition. We shared a common secret—how to heal from the inside. We partook of the same medicine, self-administered.

If each of us grows our emotional wounds in personal ways, scarring on the inside, beyond the reach of a physician's stethoscope, then how fitting it is that we summon our own healing balm from the great and indefatigable depths within, too.

My father is a Vietnam Veteran. He told me once that his childhood home was so beautiful, but also so terrifying, that the jungles and noise and sweat of the war felt relaxing to him. Besides, he had already cultivated a secret weapon to survive the bullets and the terror: his guitar and pen.

I have heard the tapes my father made during the war, guns reporting outside his dwelling while he sang the songs of his soul. His young voice like a spark being fanned by an internal, unlimited source.

It was a long, imperfect climb out of the jungle, to marriage, to being a single father raising my two brothers and I. And it was no fairy tale. Words like 'trauma' and 'triggering' were not on the horizon for decades. But even through the booze and the women, I witnessed my father keeping himself alive, his pen and his paper always nearby.

I learned from him. I never picked up the bottle. But I did pick up the pen and marveled at the undeniable truth of such an act—for at that moment I became the patient and the healer. My thin skin encompassed a power that was palpable. Even I, at my tender age, with my limited education, could be transformed by that gaze turning inward, where grace would take over, helping me to arrange syllables and consonants into shapes that would be a balm to the injuries no one else could see.

I could form sentences, pointed and metallic, and thrust them into my own heart, to push away the bitter pain. Of course, I thought, of course Nature would not leave us each stranded, alone. Of course we would each have access not only to the pain, but the cure. Of course we would each have the ability to sit and soften and unfold the creased places. Untangle our nerves. Participate in a living archeological dig, gently removing the mud and hurt and violence one syllable at a time, to once again see the North Star of the simple truths that comprise our DNA, and lean upon them, sure as bones.

I have heard the old stories, of the old ways. How each warrior was bathed and placed in the salt caves, wrapped in mud, and asked to rest until their nerves unwound. Their burden draining from them, back into the capable earth. I have heard the old stories, and how our healers knew what to do with pain. Somewhere between the unconscionable conquering of our indigenous brothers and sisters and lighting a candle at the altar of technology, we forgot how to heal. But I take comfort in the inextinguishable knowledge that lives in each of us. Writing is the Shaman's call, leading us inward, dreaming in feverish states, to find the closed places, and beckon in the light.

My dad is seventy-three now. And his own words guided him through his sobriety and whispered to him how to heal. Just like they did for me. And what you will read in these pages is the same miracle. You are witnessing the healing of souls.

COMMUNITY BUILDING ART WORKS

# *I.*

*You do not have to be me in order for us to fight alongside each other. I do not have to be you to recognize that our wars are the same. What we must do is commit ourselves to some future that can include each other and to work toward that future with the particular strengths of our individual identities. And in order to do this, we must allow each other our differences at the same time as we recognize our sameness.*

—Audre Lorde

# Faisal Mohyuddin

## Because Seeking Can Help a Person Be Found, And Because First They Must Learn How to Seek

*for Seema Reza and the CBAW community*

Some days, we wake, our hearts unwell, heavy clouds dimming

    Every bright thought's bright refulgence, rendering our bodies

        Empty, unrested, ache-ridden, and scant. Yet, we know we must

Mask the pain, upcast ourselves, shoulder through the storms, find

    Another source of light toward which to turn our faces—and learn to

        Rely on seeking to lessen the blight, to discover the gifts of

Energy and hope that take the shape of dear friends like you.

    Zillions of people on this hard, brutal earth, yet only some who

        Act like a steadfast sun, whose radiant giving guides us through.

COMMUNITY BUILDING ART WORKS

# Let Memory Graze

*Usually*
*I let my memory graze on its own ...*
*To forget the wound and remember the knife.*

—Qassim Haddad, tr. Khaled Mattawa

# Mahogany L. Browne

## Redbone Dances

If you ain't never watched your parents kiss
        ain't neva have them teach you
'bout the way lips will      to bend & curve
against a lover's affirmation

If you ain't never watched the knowing nod
of sweethearts worn away & soft
as a speaker box's blown out hiss

If you ain't witnessed the glue
that connected your mother & father
—how they fused their single selves
into the blunt fist of parents

If you ain't sure there was a time when
their eyes held each other like a nexus
breaking the lock to dip dark marbles
into certain corners of a shot glass

If you ain't never known a Saturday night
slick with shiny promises & clouds
wrapped wet in a Pendegrass croon

If you ain't been taught how
a man hold you close      *so close*
...it look like a crawl

If you ain't had the memory
of your mother & father sliding
hip to hip      Their feet whisper
a slow shuffle & shift      Her hand
on his neck grip the shoulder of
a man that will pass his daughters
bad tempers      & hands like bowls

If you ain't watched a man
lean into a woman His eyes
a boat sliding across bronze
        His hands

pillared in her auburn hair     Her
throat         holds   the urge

to hear how her voice sounds against
the wind of him

If your skin can't fathom the heat
of something as necessary as this…

Then you can't know the hurricane
of two bodies   how   the bodies
can create the prospect of a sunrise
how that sunrise got a name
        it sound like: a blues song;
a woman's     heart *breaking*;
From the record player skipping
        the sky       almost

blue

# Shana Turner

## Poem for Bill Withers [a record of April 4, 2020]

*prompted by Seema Reza*

It has been five days since Bill Withers passed away.

Today I sang his songs from the steps of my porch.
My neighbor, a dear friend
who is the closest physical contact I've had
during these days of quarantine,
sang from the chair on her porch next door.

Today I watched military tanks roll
on the train tracks that run
two blocks down from my house.

Today the number of human
lives claimed by the treachery
which has allowed this virus to flourish
totals one-hundred and fifty-three
in the city of New Orleans alone.

Today I cannot speak
to my friend who is incarcerated
because they've been put on lockdown
in their cells
until further notice.

Today I mash ginger with turmeric and honey.
I squeeze limes inside my palms
and sprinkle the juice with cayenne pepper.
I watch the swirl of sunset gold blend
as I pour the medicine into a glass bottle of maroon,
Hibiscus-steeped tea.

Today I feel sacredness in the ritual
of filling and refilling a small jar with water,
pouring it into the pots that line
my kitchen window sills,
whispering for the tiny vegetable seedlings
and young aloe to grow.

Today I feel sacredness in the ritual
of removing my shoes by the front door
as I cross over the threshold between
the world outside
and the inner space of home.

The sacredness in the ritual of
mopping the floors,
washing my clothing,
and my hands,
and the countertops;

as I bathe in eucalyptus, rosemary, saltwater
prepared by my neighbor,
my dear friend
who is the closest physical contact I've had
during these days of quarantine.

I hear the piano chords as we sing his words:

*Sometimes in our lives we all have pain,*
*we all have sorrow.*
*But if we are wise, we know that there's*
*always tomorrow.*

# Anthony Almojera

## 13 Bodies [a day in the life of a pandemic paramedic]

*prompted by Seema Reza*

What is a soul to someone who
Watches them depart like flights out of JFK?

Red and blue lights,
Sirens wailing
Families sobbing.
Medics with their thousand yard stare
PPE hopefully protecting them from catching feelings.

All that they were,
All they will ever be,
All things are now equal.
As they lay agape,
Maybe for the first time their eyes wide open.

We remove the tube as his last spit drips off.
His last remaining healthy microbes fleeing trying to find refuge from what is to come.
Bearing witness not knowing what to do and what I was exactly trying to save.
Wipe off the equipment as another flight leaves for its mysterious destination.

I remove my glasses thankful for the blurriness...

# Hari Alluri

## Blessing Wednesday

Bless the dreams that let me ease rare
into my waking, the miracle of stress
wafting as the cat's tail to her bowl. Bless the third time
out the front door. Bless the cafe's chocolate
croissants that didn't make it in, the barista's 6am
cheeky laugh at my, "guess I'll take
this misery with me as I go." Bless
my failed attempts at grace, bless the final
giving in to dancing later as I cut
another lawn, bless the tired hour—extending
a slightly shorter day, a sun that doesn't
quite break through the clouds
at highest noon. Bless big
tune behind big tune. Bless the casual
single backup to the trailer, the fall-in
hitch, the ditch I miss, the worm I miss it by,
the ever-loving earth I hit to stretch
my trimmer line, to free dirt of my boots, getting
a little closer to anywhere I have to go. Bless and bless
the co-worker who reads my mind and throws me
keys, the one who leaves a mess
I have to clean, the one who snarks
the second one to make the first one laugh. Bless
I've been all three. Bless bucket and rake, bent
machine and hole in tarp. Bless
I'll get right on it. Bless unwanted,
the definition of weeds. Bless living's
sometimes gentle greed. Bless horsetail,
rhizome root, the sideways
and the deep, indigenous refusal
to be uprooted. Bless the healing in the leaf
I've never used, the effortlessness
I cultivate, the lie of effortless. Bless the brown
woman at the Chevron till, bless she
slept enough, bless, while I fill my coffee cup,
our under-banter, our at-racism jabs. Bless brake
pedal, bless petal, bless pollen like a snowdrift, the lighter
I don't bless it with, the sneezes I do. This city refusing to bless

the ground with any cherry trees but male: a widespread
policy of no free food: this patriarchy of taming: of grow
what takes and take what grows: of uproot the low: of keep
the love of nature from over-springing forth: bless it
into something else. The pain the city causes, bless
with liniment, bless with horsetail salve
all our muscle ache and sweat, bless
the epicentre, bless fractured caress.

# Jason Magabo Perez

## Beneath These Hands

*prompted by Hari Alluri / after Arthur Kayzakian & the CBAW brainstorm*

This aesthetic of intellect beneath
these hands, these hands beneath

running water. This woman, this
singing woman, this singing and

singed cartography. You are here
to disarticulate body from voice,

a materiality of dilemma—yes,
so singular. You demand prose

that stains heart and lung, a hand
that fails form. You, thorough

haunting, drying mud lodged in
your fingernails, are here tonight.

And tonight, let children run, let
them gently tear into night, let them

imagine, too, what it is to be torn
through a lyric of expired want.

# Arthur Kayzakian

## Translation

*prompted by Hari Alluri / after the CBAW brainstorm*

as in the night that wrecked my hands, a city of crows daggered through the sky. as in a skull of complex nightmares, the black owl of my mouth, a box of dreams for strangling. as in hope, as in my mother's voice, as in we avoided the mouth of a door forced open. as in the quiet voice of god crashing through the lifeless, a separation: animal from spirit. from kentanee to hokee. as in salt turns an ocean nocturnal with its smallness. the night between us has a restless gap. as in birds flutter. as in cage, as in a wild hive of prayers under my breath. as in we live just one more breath with segments of light. as in we live in a city dragged to the sea by the hands of its night. as in the sugar of a dying language, the scent of ash and a bashed in door. as in smoke-rings blown from the mouth of a glorified general. as in river then a slice of jail. of wine stain, the torture of praying. as in history. as in we wait with white men for metal doors to slide open. as in instead of anger, we have flower petal weight on our shoulders. as in psychedelic. it's okay we smile. it's not okay we know: as in more red than music, more curtains dropped on our homes than nightfall. as in memory. as in the threaded rasp of my mother's voice cloaks the siren, she walks closer to me ever slowly dropping parts of her dark sky. as in instead of radio, a ghost picks up a stream, a frequency foreign to the ear. as in we are foreign stones who have turned to wishes without promise. as in we flee. we dance, moonwalk angle in our shadows. as in we fall. as in we fall through our mother's lies for safety. as in we live beneath the yellow death of sun, our language: a summer bomb mixed with extinction. as in i was delivered from war when my mother fired up the lie barricaded in her breast to save me. as in bandana. as in these days I feel ill-gotten, which is to say i'm rugged, as in I stare hard at a painting before I take it with me, as in my friends call me the armenian-persianist, as in an immigrant with a junkyard smile. as in my friends dress like wolves. as in joy has been swept to an aftermath of bodies, mangled. as in ill. as in cough from the small of my delicate sun. as in touch. as in we locked lips under the flicker of lights in a dim-walled hallway. as in my crime is not so much in denying my hunger, but the great extent i went to hide my ability for loss. as in the war. as in on us. as in the nights a city howls in honor of its body count. as in the cemetery has grown jealous of the city, and the evening tucked in its blade so the sunset could live.

# Rachelle Cruz

## The You

*prompted by Hari Alluri / after a reading a fragment of Toni Morisson's Jazz / after Steven Universe's Lion*

The you who absorbs children into your pinkness,
Your pink halo and circuitry for a meadow-kind
place for running, or plucking grass and saying I'm sorry.
The you who is a mother's shard, pinked with pain.
There are so many yous you've lied about only
because you weren't safe with the fullness of your selves.
The you who yawned with glowing eyes and vestiges
of a mother's sumac memory --
a beachball, a sword, a knowing how to fight.
What part of you is a mother, a lion scratching the sand.
The you of forgiveness, of detached regard,
The you of selective hearing, of disappearing tenderness,
of sugared breath combing through your child's hair.
The you of another portal in which falling isn't a destination.
How this you cries with an openness to be heard.
The you in mint, the you in ochre, the you in stunning
tanbark splinters, the you crystallized with all of your knowing,
the you with the leftovers is the secret to time.

# Brenda Johnson

## We Were Never Taught Anything About Love Except "Jesus Loves Me"

*prompted by Seema Reza / after Shin Ji Moon*

Words of love do not pass through
stiff upper lips pursed against pain
of bearing children and its lifelong aftermath

Hands do not touch in caring caresses
but knead the sticky bread dough and
pass on photos, recipes, and land

Minds focussed on survival, profits, and what people will say
have no time for whatever love is
after youth's short-lived surge of hormones

# Martha E. Pedersen

## How to Feed the Black Bears

*prompted by Amelia Bane*

In order to attract black bears, you must make your yard appealing and fun. Many people find bears attracted to their homes and yards without invitation and go to great lengths to dissuade them. However, if you want them there, follow these simple steps.

Step 1. Generate edible garbage. Fish skeletons work well. So does old hamburger, cooked or not. Make sure it's smelly. Bears don't like flower-scented food. Anything with honey is good. Start raising bees in the back yard. The bears will attack the hive and eat the yellow dripping honey while being attacked by bees. Maple syrup might work too. It's beautifully sweet—but only the real stuff. Not that maple-flavored corn syrup that tries to pass itself as real syrup. It's sweet and it might attract bears. However, for the discerning maple syrup snob, and you should be one, it fails.

Be aware: if you have a sugaring operation, bears have a sweet tooth and are crafty. If you're not careful, and even if you are, you might find a syrupy mess one morning. Proper safeguards are required. Bears don't pay for what they eat.

Step 2. Make the garbage accessible. The local dump is a great place for bears—a veritable smorgasbord of refuse. A black bear's favorite. Lacking a dump in your neighborhood, or even your back yard, you could create one. However, calling it a compost pile won't fool the neighbors or the health department. That's too easy for bears anyway. Bears like to play and investigate. A bear-proof bin will guarantee they'll look for food in other places. Like your unlocked car after a trip to the grocery. I hear they like cheese and crackers.

No composting? Buy a pair of 31-gallon galvanized steel trash cans with side handles. Don't forget the lid with the center handle and a couple of bungee cords, all sold separately. To secure the lid, attach one end of the bungee cord to one side handle on the can, run it through the handle on the lid, and attach it to the other can handle. This secures the lid from most scavengers and the wind while giving you easy access for filling. Bears find trying to separate the lid from the can great fun. Don't be surprised if they play a version of "kick the can" leaving claw marks and impact dents on the can and lid. They will get the lid off and enjoy whatever goodies you left for them. Make sure it was worth it. Who knows? Your mangled can might end up two or three houses away.

Step 3. Get your mangled cans back from wherever the bears left them. Check your neighbor's yards as well. If they're not bear friendly, I suggest you sneak over before dawn to avoid being seen and remove any evidence. They heard the ruckus during the night and will be greatly displeased to find their yard trashed. Clean up what remnants the bears left behind and get them to the dump or ready for pickup.

Step 4. Repair your cans. Knock out the dents. Cover the holes the bear claws made during their rumpus hour with duct tape. Don't try to be fancy and play with the tape color. Basic silver duct tape is best. By the end of the month, you'll need a new can, so don't put too much art into mending. The bear's aesthetic doesn't lean that way.

Step 5: Replenish the edible garbage. Fill the can as before, leave it outside in a bear accessible area, and wait. Who knows? If you leave good eats they might bring a friend or two next time.

SUGGESTION: Make sure your home security system or motion active cameras film and record at night in hi-def. You will need this for your entertainment and for your kid's Show and Tell or science class. You could enter your favorite bear escapades in Funniest Home Animal Videos and win money. If the bears become a nuisance, your local Fish and Wildlife service can offer relocation. Do what you can to avoid that. You'd have to wait for a while before starting with other bears or less desirable raccoons.

WARNING: Bears might look cute and cuddly, especially the cubs, but they are NOT pets. Mama bear won't like you playing with them. Keep your distance or you might end up looking like your garbage can.

# Kate Lewis

## Becoming

*prompted by Seema Reza / after Ellen Bass*

Let me tell you what it was like, to feel like this was everything.
We plan to make French onion soup.
He arrives while I'm chopping onions.
While they caramelize —
that hour when they become gorgeous
— we walk to the harbor for a smoke.

I wear my raincoat.
Crumbled bits of bud grind permanently
into the seams of my pockets.

It should have been Marathon Monday,
the twentieth of April,
half past the hour.
It's cool and cloudless, a little raw,
but mercifully the rain has passed.
The sky shines lapis over the Greenway.

It should have been packed.
I picture ghosts:
sinewy runners wrapped up in silver blankets,
surrounded by loved ones,
toasting a triumph.
The Hanover Street bistros are still shuttered.
If you listen hard, the silence is taunting.


A vintage car, a brilliant aquamarine Cadillac,
is parked on the street in the North End
outside the improv theater.
A man on the street is freestyle rapping.
We stop to listen.

COMMUNITY BUILDING ART WORKS

# Raychelle Heath

## If We Could Once Upon a Time

*prompted by Joe Merritt / After Yusef Komunyakaa*

Once we carried mini bags of gun powder to smash against the concrete to make the loudest sound, one that would drown out our celebratory laughter

Once you handed me a poem about a wolf, and I wrapped it in a snakeskin, braced it with silver wire and an amethyst stone and wore it at my throat as a talisman

Once I gathered short tufts of my hair, twisting each between my fingers before donning it with a shell until my head was like a shake-a-ray, I the dancer, I the drum

Once I sat in a workshop and hammered silver into the four directions, into butterfly wings, into pure prana, into us

Once we were kids once we were friends once we were lovers once we were released

Once a fork traded for a spoon, something rounder fuller smoother, we could feed each other without threat

Once you gave the moon and I howled with delight and we remembered ourselves into river into song into the belly of a shell

# Faisal Mohyuddin

## Ghazal for the Diaspora

We have always been the displaced children of displaced children,
Tethered by distant rivers to abandoned lands, our blood's history lost.

To temper the grief, imagine your father's last breath as a Moghul garden—
Marble pool at its center, the mirrored sky holding all his tribe had lost.

Above the tussle of his wounded city, sad-eyed paper kites fight to stay aloft.
One lucky child will be crowned the winner, everyone else will have lost.

Wish peace upon every stranger who arrives at your door, even the thief—
For you never know when your last chance at redemption will be lost.

In another version of the story, a steady loneliness mothers away the rust.
Yet, without windows in its hull, the time-traveler's supplication gets lost.

Against flame-lipped testimonies of exile's erasures, the swinging of an axe.
Felled banyan trees populate your nightmares, new enlightenments lost.

The rim of this porcelain cup is chipped, so sip with practiced caution.
Even a trace of blood will copper the flavor, the respite of tea now lost.

Tell me, Faisal, with what new surrender can you evade deeper damnation?
Whatever it is, hack away, before your children too become the Lost.

# Ruby Singh

## Between Ribs and Courage

*prompted by Hari Alluri / after Faisal Mohyuddin*

We have always been the descendants of the citrine hallow
Filtering between the branches of knowing cedar and imagining winds
Guiding lights of the mirror calling itself back to self

Extending palms holding the spine between ribs and courage
Lifting what's needed and letting the weight settle
into what gravity will hold for you

We have always been the boat adrift on a shadow filled sea
Our mast pointing towards the home of our ancestors
The reflection always runs true and straight through

Bio illuminated lanterns of the great uncoiling
The tethered ends of a ruby dress that has been whirling in ecstasy
before memory gave you a name
the grandmothering of prayer

We have always been the bare foot on the dusty path
Tracing the lines etched by the many and known to the few
Dot to dot drawing constellations
between the movement of our hearts

# Ruth Christopher

## On Tuesdays We Go to Senator Jones

*prompted by Hari Alluri / after Faisal Mohyuddin*

To temper the grief, imagine your heart palpitations as you approach the security guard presiding over this short chunk of Santa Monica sidewalk. The walls of the building he's guarding throb because Charlie always turns up the god damn bass too high. Imagine his nod as he undoes the velvet rope to let you pass without checking your ID.

"How's the big man?"

"He's good, smoking hookah tonight."

"Tell him I say hi."

One door swings open and then the other—men love opening doors for me at salsa night, they think it improves their odds of dancing with me. I suppose it does. I enter the sauna of decadent joy that is Senator Jones proper and am immediately accosted by Eddie Palmieri at 150 decibels along with sweat, cologne, a chaotic movement that takes no notice of me. I grin as I hand my $10 bill to someone with a money box at the door. She mouths something, I have no idea what because you can't hear shit over the music.

I thread my way through a short staircase of leering men with drinks. Gaining the platform, I choose to enjoy rather than resent their stares. Not so many white bitches in salsa. I sit down, switch my shoes, hide my things under a table creaking under the weight of empty glasses, then go to the DJ booth to kiss Charlie.

From there I can survey both floors and the bar for any of my personal threats: A—, who I was never able to get a restraining order against. E—, who I'm not too keen on ever since he tried to shove me in his car in the parking structure at Rain. Poodle Poop who's just a pain in my ass. Ditto Momma J. Enrique who—well, I don't want to get into it. I control my trembling hands as I see A— dancing with a blond tourist on the far side of the floor. She must not know. I make my way for the bar. *¿Quieres bailar conmigo?* Usually Mango just tickles me or pulls my ear. I kiss his cheek and we take to the floor.

# Elizabeth Hassler

## Krill

*prompted by Hari Alluri / after Faisal Mohyuddin*

To temper the grief, imagine
the body alighted. Imagine
the colors close tints under your knuckles
(white), your hunger, handing throating eyeing
—trust your overhang to taste & know your
thirst, your first, your recent bursted skin.
What do you want? Where is your mouth?

The mouth at the base of your spine
will say: we are what really happened.

Or no, we aren't. We are
the hung-between.
We are what clothes hangers come for.

When we have clothed you, enough,
will you rip up the story that tells
who baked gas gap in the sheet cake of your
spine? That's why a mouth
lives there, to fulfill promise
surrounding owned sweetness
& fizz, pop, umami hiss. You are a baleen whale,
sifting through lakes you've undrowned in,

unvolcanoes & all your unavoided breaths
for fragments you can eat to temper the grief.
Imagine your spine! Alighted, promised:

all birthday-candle come-through;
come-true; measure heat mouth, mouth trill,
till mouth, still mouth, mouth thrill exacted shiny.
What do you know
about tempering?

# Your Own Gestures and Symbols

*Do you accept your own gestures and symbols? Do you believe what you yourself say? When you act, do you believe what you are doing?*

—Muriel Rukeyser

# Jennifer Patterson

## What I Know

*prompted by Hari Alluri / after Faisal Mohyuddin*

What I know is that I don't know. I no longer care to clarify, sanctify, make "sense".

I can not give language to this.

I root down into

the space of not knowing. I root down. Let the veils of eyes close.

The less I cling to knowing, the more alive I feel, the more shot through space I feel

and there's comfort there, in this not knowing, this space travel, this otherworldly drift, this erratic ether.

No more performing "being the one with the answer". I have no answers. Will you sit in the questions with me? Will you?

But back to magic.

In the sand.
Stretched across mountains.
Nestled in the ice drippings on the juniper trees.

We try to wrestle power away from those who claim magic but only seem concerned with destruction

but destruction is magic too.

The way we cling to what needs to rot, is there magic there too? Or is it only magic when we loosen our grip, slam back into the not knowing, of no clarity on what will take its place.

There is no way out.

We die, we come back, we die, we come back. we die. We come back?

Swallowed by sand and mountains and branches of a juniper outstretched,

let the edges of this life, the trappings, the hard shell fall away

and we are, once again, a spore, a cell, hurtling towards birth.

# Tiffany Nicole Fletcher

## One Thing I Know

*prompted by Jennifer Patterson / after Leah Horlick*

Periwinkle blue bird whose
song a low peaceful sigh,
made a visitation yesterday—
came to my windowsill
came to me
gave me a melody.
Healing came by surprise,
carried on the wind—
to me—floating on wings;
without any effort on my part.
After all my searching,
one thing I know is this:
the remedy we seek can be found.

# Joan Smith Green

## Ain't Nothin' But A Thang

*prompted by Amelia Bane*

Cecelia has a blanket fetish. She acquires blankets from hospital ERs, patient rooms, and laundry carts. Cecelia has a special zippered bag just for hospital visits. It is a gorgeously detailed Vera Bradley bag with pale yellows, purples, and greens in a flowered paisley pattern. No one ever questions the bag. It always appears stuffed when she enters and equally stuffed when she exits.

No one suspects that Cecelia is a kleptomaniac. She steals one or more blankets every time she goes to any hospital. She empties her overstuffed Vera Bradley bag of the multitude of plastic grocery bags and refills it with every blanket she can find. She quite calmly exits the hospital with her ill-gotten treasures.

At home she carefully inspects each blanket for stains, rips, or other imperfections. She mends, patches, and washes them with great attention to detail. Late into the night, her preprogrammed Singer Sewing Machine embroiders a lovely yellow rose and the words *Sleep tight, my friend* on every blanket. She gently wraps each blanket in brown paper and string.

Every week, Cecelia visits different facilities and drops off each package for a sick child, an elderly citizen, a veteran, a cancer patient, a foster child, or a homeless person.

She never signs her work.

She steals to give away.

# Miden Wood

## Advice for Those Whose Moth Got Out

*prompted by Jon Sands / after Nazim Hikmet / after Claudia Rankine*

Don't gulp,
Don't gulp!
Don't let him hear your cartoon fear.
Part of you may want to mend the hole that appeared in your pants late Monday
After you closed the moth into a zipper pocket
Of your cargo shorts
good for all keeping but the keep-him-from-chewing kind,
but the keep-him-from-going kind.

Instead
Rent a go-cart and floor it around the loop, right through that cloud of summer gnats
You will like the feeling of their bodies hitting your face
And they will like the feeling of your face hitting their bodies
And it will all serve as a reminder that you are as big as
at minimum
like a thousand gnats.

When the moth knocks your lamp off the end table, don't say "I'm right," don't say
    "you're right."
Instead, eat popcorn for dinner and make peace with the moth's concussion-love for a
    bright irresistible.
And as you seam-rip the holy pocket out,
consider how violently the moth loves a bulb,
and reckon it was pretty vicious to gulp him into your cargo pants in the first place,
zipped up in an unspoken dark.

# Jim Tritten

## I Am From

*prompted by Seema Reza / after George Ella Lyon*

I am from ... a time that no longer exists,

It used to exist, but most of us who could remember that time no longer are here,

Or can no longer remember,

It was a time of growth as I learned what it would take to move forward and adjust with time as it advanced,

It was a time of safety nurtured by loving grandparents,

And a grandmother who could cook toast, haluska, and chicken better than I have ever experienced anywhere since,

And a grandfather who took me to Ebbets Field to watch the Brooklyn Dodgers,

It was the time of my first girlfriends,

Girlfriends because at the age of six, I had two,

My mother asked me what we should name my new sister,

That's how my sister became Susan Janet,

It was a time to make lifelong friends and never worry about their politics,

It was a time to stretch and explore,

I earned the rank of Eagle Scout and am still proud of that achievement,

I had great scout leaders who served as excellent role models,

It was a time to learn that giving back and sharing was not just expected but good for society,

I learned about karma later,

I am from a time when a President spoke to us and said not to ask what your country can do for you but what you can do for your country,

I am from a time when volunteering for the military was expected, appreciated, something to be proud of,

and I am from a time when those who had other opinions about the military threw raw eggs on my uniform as I visited a campus on a recruiting tour of duty, a time when no one ever said thank you for your service,

when everyone I knew used racial or ethnic slurs,

when many things taken for granted today were illegal,

when I ate mustard sandwiches because we could not afford baloney,

I am from ... a time that no longer exists.

# cd ybarra

## [I am from...]

*prompted by Seema Reza / after George Ella Lyon*

I am from nowhere and everywhere, itinerant traveler without
a home

I am from shame and cowardice, incest and alcohol, built up and
torn down

I am from San Diego East County, Chicano Park. The ugly duckling to California's
bronzed and beautiful

I am from Christmas Eve Tamales and whole pig bodies wrapped in banana leaves
cooked in the ground like traditions passed

I am from pathological holy rollers, John Birch, burned books, carried out in my own
backyard

I am from the streets of Omaha, St. Katherine Siena, St. Francis of Assisi, my guardian
angels, saints among saints.

I am from holy family, little sisters of mercy.

I am from Dolores. Dolor is pain in Spanish.

I am from Ft. Leonard Wood, Ft. Sam, Ft. Bliss, Conn Barracks. Sisterhood and
discipline run through my veins.

I am from the earth, flesh and blood, from dust to dust again.

# Cynthia Dewi Oka

## Pastoral in Which a Deer's Thirst is the Tragic Hero

Years ago, I walked just like this, from a town's one end
to the other under a church's bouquet of fire. It sang

through its steeple, of the deer's longing for the stream and mine
for something I couldn't name, something like a throat

of white silk, like the gown my mother bought for me
from a secondhand store hours before she gave the doctors

permission to unhook my father from the machines.
The walk I'm thinking of is not that final one

toward the worry lines of the hospital, though cars passed by
just like this, with shadows inside wrapped tightly around

their own plots; the metal and glass pretending to protect them
from the wind's agendas and the deer seeking water

on the other side of the road. I've learned through
sheer repetition to go in a specific direction without a plan

for how to survive. Now, as then, warnings in the periphery:
a rake's waxed tines by the hardware store's entrance,

a field throbbing with boy-pride and sweat, the white dashes
of a broken road. A deer put in motion by desperation defies

all these orders. Come here. Cease and desist. Do not. Pieces
of the sky fall like leaves on a dry streambed. The church

begins to hiss and fall away. Underneath, an abandoned cinema,
shiny black bones, rows of seats packed so tightly

even as a child I had to hug my knees to fit in. I wish I could tell
this story like someone who believes in anything, for instance,

that the journey ends with a room of blue ribbons.
He said, "Kneel," and I did. My mind a white gown

caught in his antlers. From this distance, you could read it
as a sign of surrender to the plotlines authored by

poverty and dead grass. I couldn't turn away. Metal on metal,
metal on flesh, flesh in flesh. His cinematic rage, reels of it,

in the clicking brightness. When it was spent, I walked back, hiding
my wounds from the church my father had built with his hands

and placed over my head with love, with what I must believe
was love. I wish I could have named the riches I passed

on my way – the human doubts, the red in a cemetery of apples.
"Kneel," he said, and pushed my head into the ashes.

The sun on my back was my audience, though I couldn't
hear it, what I felt, behind the water scrubbing cold

over my thighs. What could have been language appeared
as a gown ripped from my arms mid-bloom. My mother lying

on her side, turned toward the empty half of the bed.
You understand – I had to save the life I was ashamed to live.

Now here I am, walking with a deer's instinct for water,
one drought to the next, sorrow's repeating center

cut out of its premise, its aftermath.

# Joy Jacobson

## Praise: A Cento

*after Joy Harjo / Gathered from the CBAW Crew's affirmation chat on September 9, 2021*

Praise the dark
the myriad stars
the myriad stars, the milky way
Valhalla
praise the path into self
grounding flight
empty praise come on
because it's expected...
echoes in heart chambers
some people refuse peace
the path that unfolds beneath your feet
And the things you have lost control of
praise the uncertainty
praise... the things you have lost control of!
the uncertainty
will be given to your granddaughter's goldfish
Tell me!
Like a traffic cone
Like the light was never prepared
in the morning it seems like the light never knew us
let me/ out
into the sunset of the whole world
let me out rhythm
you are made for apocalypse
the cat can stay inside angry
ready to go like a racing flag
not yet
maybe, maybe, maybe
let it be okay even if it doesn't feel good
Baby cry of a wake
wet around his raccoon eyes
the angel name
you are feeling what the world is holding
I can't say I'm an addict, but I'm doing too much
Color of my son
cherish the not burning
The drop like we hear in music

He leaves in a gust
ashes ashes keep falling down
praise the path that brought you here. bungee cord
A mother never knows ... holding or letting go
a mother never knows.
a love letter to a burning world
the clay we curl into bowls to hold our grapes
bones in these pruny pods
Just little beans
praise the sauntering path
when you hear a noise in the woods it is you
in this lusher place
praise the eggs you will lay then...
It always managed to rain right under your feet
footstep hunting
Or outside of the bed
creates the anxiety of monsters  under the bed
unless it returns
Of fear of falling asleep
the darkness of the night becomes comforting again
beautiful.
such a sweet ending
A second heartbeat beside you
blackberries, yes!
praise the brambles!
and the bees!
something keeps me going on
I'll be alone
A safe heart
When I love myself I'll have a safe heart
So I could just know and move on
if your house is not a home then where do you belong?
The baby cry through the wall in the early morning
The gentle name, the moon name
where the car waits to carry me
when I am being enough
When I am being enough

The way I speak them back
grace, it brings more grace
the moon name I call myself when I am being enough
Praise the light that never fails
the places I finally left
Praise it all and let it go
my legs long beneath my skin

# Courtney LeBlanc

## Praise the Dark

*prompted by Joy Jacobson / After Joy Harjo*

Praise the dark because it always
ends, the sun always rises and the black
sky always fades to purple, magenta,
blue. Sitting on the front steps, ceramic
mug warm against my palm, watching
the day wake. My father is lying
inside, the hospital bed near the window
in the living room so he can feel
the sunshine on his skin. From outside
I can't hear the rattle of his breath.
I try to enjoy the moment – the quiet
cool of morning, the sky greeting me.
Before the day is done my dad will take
his last breath but I don't know that yet.
The day will be bright and blue. My heart
will break and the sun will set. Praise the dark.

# Yesenia Montilla

## a brief meditation on breath

i have diver's lungs from holding my
breath for so long. i promise you
i am not trying to break a record
sometimes i just forget to
exhale. my shoulders held tightly
near my neck, i am a ball of tense
living, a tumbleweed with steel-toed
boots. i can't remember the last time
i felt light as dandelion. i can't remember
the last time i took the sweetness in
& my diaphragm expanded into song.
they tell me breathing is everything,
meaning if i breathe right i can live to be
ancient. i'll grow a soft furry tail or be
telekinetic something powerful enough
to heal the world. i swear i thought
the last time i'd think of death with breath
was that balmy day in july when the cops
became a raging fire & sucked the breath
out of Garner; but yesterday i walked
38 blocks to my father's house with a mask
over my nose & mouth, the sweat dripping
off my chin only to get caught in fabric & pool up
like rain. & i inhaled small spurts of me, little
particles of my dna. i took into body my own self
& thought i'd die from so much exposure
to my own bereavement—they're saying
this virus takes your breath away, not
like a mother's love or like a good kiss
from your lover's soft mouth but like the police
it can kill you fast or slow; dealer's choice.
a pallbearer carrying your body without a casket.
they say it's so contagious it could be quite
breathtaking. so persistent it might as well
be breathing            down your neck—

# Nicole Arocho Hernández [09.23.20]

## muse: muscle

*prompted by Yesenia Montilla*

at the beginning          of my thirst

a dandelion          yellow gulps of

spring          delicate

dancing          is it the wind who

brings me          words.   is   it

the drowning     who     brings me

sounds it is          the soft spot

on your collarbone          dear

that brings me back       from the dead

# Ross Gay

## ode to the puritan in me

There is a puritan in me
the brim of whose
hat is so sharp
it could cut
your tongue out
with a brow
so furrowed you
could plant beets
or turnips or
something of course
good for storing
he has not taken a nap
since he was two years old
because he detests
sloth above all
he is maybe the only real person
I've ever heard
say "sloth" or "detest"
in conversation
he reads poetry
the puritan in me
with an X-Acto knife in his calloused hand
if not a stick of dynamite
and if the puritan in me sees
two cats making
whoopee in the barn
I think not
because they get
in the way
or scare the crows
but more precisely
because he thinks it is worthless
the angles of animals
fucking freely
in the open air
he will blast them to smithereens
I should tell you
the puritan in me always carries a shotgun

he wants to punish the world I suppose
because he feels he needs punishing
for who knows how many unpunishable things
like the times as a boy he'd sneak shirtless between the cows
to haul his tongue across the saltlick
or how he'd study his dozing granny's instep
like it was the map of his county
or the spring nights he'd sneak to the garden behind the sleeping house
and strip naked
while upon him lathered the small song
of the ants rasping their tongues
across the peonies' sap, making of his body
a flower-dappled tree
while above him the heavens wheeled and his tongue
drowsed slack as a creek,
on the banks of which, there he is,
right now, the puritan in me
tossing his shotgun into the cattails,
taking off his boots, and washing his feet
in that water.

# Jennifer A. Minotti

## Go, You are Not Welcomed

*prompted by Yesenia Montilla / after Ross Gay*

To the nag in the crown of my head who unrelents.
Who will not let me forget every mistake I have made.
Every person who has betrayed me.
Every dishonesty that wronged.

Go. Go.

Please go away.
You are not welcomed anymore.

Sure you were useful.
You fed my ego so I could escape.
You humbled me to return home.
But I no longer need you. I no longer want you.

Go. Go.

      Go now and be gone.
      Let me live my life with the answers you gave my questions.

I promise to welcome you back when I have more questions.

      For now, let me sleep.
      Let me enjoy the fruits of your labor.
      The time you spent holding me, lecturing me, teaching me.

You learned also. There is no denying that. You cried.

So Go. Go.

      Please go away until I invite you back.
      Until then, your job is complete.

# Shuly Xóchitl Cawood

## Letter to the Children of the Future

*prompted by Caryn Mirriam-Goldberg*

You can't see the blue bird box out my window.
I don't know whether this blue bird box will exist,
or any bird boxes, or any birds. I want to tell you
to believe in them, but you might not know what I mean,
so let me start here: a bird can be small and light,
with beak and wings, feathers and clawed feet. A little
beating heart, eyes that do not blink. Birds build nests
in branches, bushes, in gutters and eaves.
I'd like to think a bird can build a nest anywhere,
taking fallen twig and bits of string, discarded
pieces, soft and hard pieces, things that can bend
and be given new life.

I want to tell you to be a bird, but you might not know
what it means to fly. You might not have wings.
You might not know what words can build
soft places in the world. You might not know
how to sing.

# Anne R. Z. Schulman

## All They Have

*prompted by Shuly Xóchitl Cawood / after Ira Sukrungruang*

You are different. You feel it deep inside. Straddling two worlds is confusing, but you don't understand how to make it right. All you know is that your parents are sad; you breathe ash.

Your first home, straight from New York Harbor, is in a dense Brooklyn neighborhood. Starting school, class sizes are always over thirty and you get no special attention from teachers.

You are invited to a classmate's sixth birthday party. At first, you feel that the invitation is a wonderful sign that you are being accepted by the American girls. You are very aware that as an immigrant, non-English speaking child, you stand apart, but you try so hard to fit in.

As the date of the party nears, you begin having feelings of trepidation. After all, such an event is a first-time experience for you. What could you expect? Oh well, you think to yourself in Yiddish, you've gotten used to learning on your feet.

Your mother walks the two blocks with you, holding your hand crossing streets, arriving at the address where Linda Weingarten lives five floors up. As parents and children are already tromping up the stairs, your mother tells you to follow the others. There are no elevators in any of the tenements, even those with as many as six floors. Your mother just nods at the other parents, gives you a pat on the tush, and promises to be waiting to pick you up on the front stoop in an hour or so. A good thing about America is that you feel safe playing on the streets.

The first disappointment you have is a familiar one; the girls are wearing special pretty frilly pastel-colored dresses. You have none, so you are still wearing your plaid woolen pleated skirt with suspenders, opaque brown stockings and your one pair of scuffed laced shoes.

You are puzzled by the colorfully wrapped boxes each child carries. What were those for? All you know is that you have none. You hold back tears of embarrassment and strangeness, attempting to cope by twirling your mousy-colored, rubber-banded braids.

When the apartment door opens, the sparkling atmosphere and decorations brighten your mood. There is Linda, in a flared pink nylon dress, your favorite color, and gracing her shoulders, a soft black velvet bolero. Her long dark twirled bottle curls are further ornamented by a pink carnation and ribbon. To you, Linda seems a fairy tale princess in the flesh.

The children dance to the record player, singing the "Hokey Pokey," "Here We "Go Loopy Loop" and "The Farmer in the Dell." You have learned these games at recess and are finally having fun. Next, you are seated at a table with pointed birthday hats at each lovely setting. Mrs. Weingarten tells everyone to hold off sounding curled blowers for a while, until after Linda has made her wish and blown out the candles atop the most beautiful, creamy, candy-rose-topped cake that you could ever imagine. After that, you try to follow the words of a song called "Happy Birthday." Linda's mother then takes orders, having offered a choice of four different ice cream flavors!

Were the doors of apartment 5C on Blake Avenue, in reality, the Gates to Heaven, you wonder. You and your sister would carefully save pennies until you had the ten cents for a Good Humor dixie cup, that actually was perhaps half a cup of ice cream, eaten with a small flat wooden "spoon." We would order the kind split into half vanilla and half chocolate, then divide it carefully crosswise so that we could each taste a bit of both flavors. We let every cool lick of sweetness melt slowly on the tongue, our eyes closed, savoring it for as long as we could. There had never been such treats in the Displaced Persons Camps of Austria and Germany.

But just before the lights are dimmed so that each candle, lit in turn, would further light up Linda's ecstatic rosy cheeked face, your little heart suddenly begins to pound. Surrounding Linda are four of her grandparents, uncles, aunts and cousins. Where are yours? You have none.

# Kendra Whitfield

## Physick

*prompted by Seema Reza / after Ellen Bass*

The women in my family swallow anger like aspirin:

> Choked down with cold coffee
> Abandoned on edges of cluttered counters,
> Forgotten during chaos.

The women in my family swallow disappointment like butter:

> On Easter Morning hot cross buns, cold slabs
> So thick they could be shards of the tomb-sealing rock,
> Souvenirs for disbelievers when salvation never comes.

The women in my family swallow fear like cheap wine:

> Cut-glass thimble goblets forced down unwilling gullets
> After Grace, before meat, never knowing
> We could say, "No."

The women in my family swallow resentment like lukewarm tea:

> Endless cups poured from leaky tin pots
> In hospital cafeterias that reek of
> Over-boiled turnips and urine-soaked sheets.

The women in my family swallow kindness like razor blades:

> Not truly meant for us -
> We accept it with  brittle smiles while the taste of blood
> Riots down our throats like a waterfall.

The women in my family swallow love like Ambien:

> Blue oblivion eclipsing consciousness,
> Releasing us from obligatory dreams,
> Granting respite but no rest.

We swallow grief like whiskey:

> Letting it rise.
> Embracing the burn.

COMMUNITY BUILDING ART WORKS

# II.

*Each writer, if [they're] lucky, is born with one important question to ask about reality, about being alive, about being human. And to the degree that [they ask] that question under the right alignment of stars, at the right place in [their] life, that question will become as urgent for us as it is for [them]. It's a mysterious thing how this happens, how the writer's quest takes on such a tremendous resonance and importance for the rest of us as well.*

—Ben Okri

# Hannah Grieco

## Release Valve

When I make bread, I focus on the feel of the dough, the windowpane test for gluten elasticity, the delicate question of adding a pinch of flour. Will it turn the mass crumbly? Will it tame the sticky webbing between my fingers?

It's a conscious decision to meditate on my baking instead of my parenting, though sometimes I look up, listening to conversations in the adjoining rooms. Is there danger? Is there crisis?

No, but my seven-year-old is perpetually angry, at her siblings or me or herself. She shouts "Ugh!" over and over, because she shaved her Barbie's head, or she hates her sister, or I've turned off the internet. "Ugh!"

Her anger is a series of short-lived spurts, fleeting explosions that diminish quickly, then spiral back up every minute, every hour, every day. I pull her to me and beg, "Please just stop saying *ugh*?"

"I know! Ugh!" she shouts in my face, then buries her whole head in my armpit.

I turn back to my bread, awkwardly kneading with one hand. I refuse to use the hook attachment on my mixer after yesterday's leaden loaf. I don't want to damage the gluten strands with the machine's lack of finesse. Or that's what I tell myself, when in reality it's the feel of the dough, a compelling squashing and flattening that simultaneously squashes and flattens the anxiety that rises in me every minute, every hour, every day. There are a thousand reasons to panic in this house, and it takes a thousand individual attempts to mask them, to not let loose on my kids or my husband or my parents, who also live here and need me.

I successfully achieve this squashing and flattening approximately 75% of the time, both with my agitation and with my kneading.

This time, I speak quietly and lovingly and my daughter, soothed, runs into the other room and immediately starts arguing with her older sister.

25% of the time I yell back when they fight, their hourly arguments like papercuts that slice over and over into skin that never seems to heal. I was an only child, adopted, and all I ever wanted was a sister. I try to remind myself of this, but I end up screaming 5% of the time, and then they silently begin their chores or run upstairs. The quiet I needed, and yet not like this.

The same happens with my bread. 25% of the time the texture is thick and hard, 5% of the time completely inedible. I blame the mixer with its unyielding hook that batters at the delicate yeast and gluten. But it's me, out-of-touch with the dough.

This time it's perfect, smooth and soft, barely pushing back as I turn and fold. I breathe out and look up to see my middle child standing in front of me. Her hands flutter and flap, a subconscious imitation of her autistic older brother's stimming. She began to do this just this past year, and I don't know if I should ignore it or gently ask her about it, or maybe just squash and flatten her hands with mine and whisper, "Shh, you're enough. I see you."

I'm afraid she'll whisper back, "No, I'm never enough. You only see him."

"Mom, mom, mom," she says instead.

"Just one second," I say and kiss her forehead. I shape the dough, not quite ready but close, into a ball and drop it in an oiled glass bowl. I cover it with plastic wrap and place it in the cool oven with the light on to proof.

This time, she is upset about something she won't tell me. She needs an hour of parental repair that I guess at, whack-a-mole style.

"You're okay. We're okay," I whisper.

She calms, mysteriously, right when I need to check my dough. It's doubled in size.

"Want to go outside?" she calls to her sister, and they're gone.

Earlier I listened to them rage-play, a release valve opening after months stuck at home. Their barbies flew, naked and wild-haired, across the dining room. They ran around the table as fast as they could, hurling their dolls back and forth and shouting at each other about toilets, body parts—anything gross or forbidden. The luxury of screaming about anuses and vaginas, collapsing, rolling around, laughing deep-belly laughs, their naked barbies attacking each other with kicks and punches.

I ignored them at the time, tried not to yell something equally inappropriate back, despite the words weighing my tongue down. Their older brother, taking a virtual class in the other room, called out, "This is ridiculous! Are you going to do something about this, mom?"

And I ignored him, too. Continued to measure out the flour gram by gram. Continued to want to shout, not to stop their play but to join it. The impulsive, almost painful need to blurt out improper words to my young children alarming, but not surprising. I don't think I have Tourette Syndrome. I don't think I have

Bipolar Disorder. I clearly have anxiety. I might have other things. My children have these and other things, too. Where do they end and I begin? Where does creativity and intelligence end, and mental illness begin? What is drive vs mania? What is existential grief vs clinical depression?

"Shut the fuck up," I whisper to my bowl of dough, before turning it out on the kitchen counter.

"Why am I such an asshole?" I've forgotten to flour the surface first. I run to the pantry, grab a handful, spill half of it on the floor, where the dog begins to lick it up. I return to the counter and realize I've grabbed confectioner's sugar instead.

"Your children all exhibit signs of Attention Deficit Disorder, as do you," the psychiatrist once said.

But where is the line between being distracted by three children who never settle into their skin and my own brain, always running, circling back on itself until I've forgotten what it means to love another person? Until life feels like a schedule I follow and nothing more?

I swap confectioner's sugar for flour. I flatten the dough, cut it in half, and reshape it into two loaves. Place them in their tins. Cover them for another proof, this time on the back counter by the coffee maker. It's warm there, draft-free.

I pour a cup of coffee from the morning carafe, room temperature now. Two hours ago, when I made this pot, my son was melting down about going to school. He hates virtual school and I don't blame him, struggle to force him to attend. But once he's logged in, he connects to others, something he didn't do at all in the year before we began this lockdown. He didn't attend school for almost six months as we tried new medications to help him want to live, as I took him out for breakfast, walked for miles trying to catch Pokémon, watched YouTube videos and pretended to laugh with him at the jokes the gamers made.

Now he panics and sobs, then logs in to school and learns about sedimentary geology, about glaciers carving out giant lakes. He discusses the history of Abrahamic religions and the relationship between religion and ancient literature. He takes notes on polynomials and non-integer exponents and asks me questions I can't answer. His head swells, the bones expanding to hold a snowballing brain.

When my son wants to live, he breathes in information and breathes out a novel, intricate origami, a thousand facts about those yelling YouTube celebrities that symbolize the low points in my life. He doesn't know that YouTube, to me, is about late nights where I hope that I can hold him tightly enough to keep him warm and breathing and mine.

I sit in the kitchen and listen to my son's online algebra class in the next room, eventually checking the loaves, which have risen almost to the top of their tins. Maybe ten more minutes. If I wait too long, they'll collapse when I score them and I'll have to start all over again.

"Mom!" he yells suddenly. "Someone's screaming!"

I rush out back, where my youngest has fallen from the swings. She clutches her arm and pushes past me.

"Ugh! I hate everybody!"

She locks herself in the bathroom.

"All my mom ever does is bake bread," I hear her brother tell his math class as I knock on the door, plead with her to let me see. "My sister almost died and she didn't even notice!"

"It wasn't my fault," my older daughter says for the millionth time.

"Yes, I know."

I offer my youngest a dollar if she'll come out of the bathroom. I offer her sister a dollar if she'll go watch a show in the basement. I head back to the kitchen, where my loaves have deflated, over-proofed and wrinkly, and my little one, uninjured, sits on the stool across from me.

"Those look gross," she says.

I dump both lumps of dough back onto the counter, which I forgot again to dust with flour. I squash them together, peel them up with a scraper, shape them into a ball and cut them in half again. I reshape them and place them in their tins by the coffee maker.

"Didn't you already do that?" my daughter asks, playing with the little ball of dough I've given her.

"I did, but now I have to fix my mistake."

"It'll be perfect, like your bread always is," she says, mimicking me, kneading and squeezing, bringing the dough to her nose and smelling it with a happy sigh.

And for just a moment, my brain slows and I recognize this feeling: love.

I put a metal pan in the oven before preheating, boil water to pour into it at the beginning of the bake. My kids like crust they can tear with their teeth.

"I want to bake bread like you," my daughter says. "One day I'll be just like you."

COMMUNITY BUILDING ART WORKS

# Let Grief

*Let grief be your sister, she will whether or no.*

—Mary Oliver

# Aracelis Girmay

## Elegy

What to do with this knowledge that our living is not guaranteed?


Perhaps one day you touch the young branch
of something beautiful. & it grows & grows
despite your birthdays & the death certificate,
& it one day shades the heads of something beautiful
or makes itself useful to the nest. Walk out
of your house, then, believing in this.
Nothing else matters.

All above us is the touching
of strangers & parrots,
some of them human,
some of them not human.

Listen to me. I am telling you
a true thing. This is the only kingdom.
The kingdom of touching;
the touches of the disappearing, things.

# Jackie Schaffner

## Triptych

*prompted by Seema Reza*

### What Sings

Beneath the top layer of earth,
the electric current of the bug world
sparks and skips with gleeful disregard
for the natural order of things.
Whatever crawls will defeat
the upright in the end.
Touch the dirt lightly:
it might be fire.

### it may be a prayer

the unused heart
expands and contracts
pulsing like a metronome
steady and clean
in its emptiness
knowing no other way
to ask to be filled—

### The frayed end of a woolen thread

remembers the sheep it came from,
feels its heart beating, still,
and wind,
and running,
water quenching thirst.
When you wear this world
on your shoulders,
let it keep you warm.
Everything we touch is alive.

# Ben Weakley

## Thirteen Times I Know You Can Hear Me

*prompted by Seema Reza / after Wallace Stevens and Adrienne Rich*

1) on the floor of a boy's blue bedroom,
   surrounded by Legos piled on the carpet
   in the form of half-assembled warplanes.

2) in a dorm room at Ithaca
   when outside is a frozen Spring night and inside is warm
   and you want to kiss her
   but will never have the courage.

3) in the twilight of the Tennessee hills
   that made you into a soldier,
   walking and whispering
   to another soldier who will be gone too soon.

4) alone in the air-conditioned trailer
   where you sit in sticky silence
   unable to cry.

5) in the sweat-stink of a Baghdad afternoon,
   where the men surround you, eager
   for meaning, yet no meaning comes
   because words are inadequate
   to fill the barren shape of death.

6) in the basement
   lit by blue light of the flickering television
   where words blur into the table
   beside a sweating glass of liquor
   that makes the ghosts who keep you company
   easier to talk to.

7) behind the wheel of your car at two-in-the-morning,
   headlights devouring the endless pavement
   and its solid yellow lines,
   when a mother's words haunt
   the man you're trying to become.

8) in the sterile cubicle where your fingers lag
   the signal from your brain

and the pen drops to the floor for a third time
and your hands will not stop shaking.

9) on the bathroom floor
   where the hot tears have finally fallen
   like the flood from the sky
   come to wash the whole earth away.

10) as you kneel before the altar
    where you light a small candle to say a prayer
    though you do not know what to pray.

11) when you've been inside all day
    because outside the world is dark and dangerous
    and some days it's better that you not go anywhere.

12) when you wake hungry for wisdom
    because you are not yet dead
    and you still have so much to give
    if only the world will have it.

13) beside the dim light of a wall-lamp,
    where you breathe in harmony with the little girl
    who is sprawled and sleep-limp across your lap
    leaving you unable to move,
    uncomfortable though you are,
    because one day she will be too old
    to rest upon you
    and that day is coming soon.

# Jon Sands

## It's a Lot

It's a lot to open your eyes in the morning,
to taste your own unbrushed mouth, to hear
thousands of voices and believe your own.
It's a lot to lose even one friend,
to not be heard, or to be heard, and still
be paranoid that people hate you. It's a lot
to put your heart on another's train tracks,
to not take a loved one hostage with your own fear,
with what you don't want to know about yourself.
Once, to explain how cold I'd become,
I confessed my love to a friend who didn't
love me back. I felt the words leave my chest,
genuine, desperate, gone. It was a lot.
ConEd bills, job applications, small talk.
A lot to shake hands, raise eyebrows, debate
about basketball, eye contact over beer.
It's a lot to hide behind a new shirt, old jeans,
to grow a beard, or eat a whole pizza,
to practice restraint, or to jog, voluntarily.
It's a lot to remember a birthday,
let alone purchase a card and mail it,
to love people as imperfect as you are.
It's a lot to not get your feelings hurt,
to let emotions pass through you,
to see your mother look like your grandmother.
It's all very necessary, but it's still a lot—
to say *I've been good* as a mannerism,
to say *I haven't* as a fact. It's a lot,
as well, to include the good things,
to not make a caricature of your sadness,
to only get your jump shot so good, and still
to have it fall left, to attend the dentist. It's a lot
to be a good husband, an inattentive uncle,
to not know how to respond—to an email—
so to say nothing. It's a lot, maybe the most,
to say nothing. Yes.
To say nothing, and therefore continue
holding that nothing inside you.
That is by far the most.

# Kim Defiori

## Reasons to Live

*prompted by Seema Reza / after Jon Sands*

It's a lot to wake up and put my uniform on
To brush away the alcohol breath
And make time for lunch

It's a lot to read emails and answer calls
To drudge home in the evenings
And eat anything but ramen and canned corn

It's a lot to stay sober at night
With the only house guests of guilt and shame
And if I'd done more, he'd be alive today

Hope is at the end of this barrel
The only true way I know to end the pain
The voices of the past are deafening
Miller Lite doesn't quiet them anymore

It's a lot to write a note explaining my end
To consider the next life
And not have to carry it anymore

Hope is pushing a magazine in the gun
Chambering a round and flicking the lever of fate
And a flood of relief as I prepare for the end
Surely these house guests won't follow me there

It's a lot to live
To breathe

Hope is my dog making his way across the room
Standing in front of me insisting I connect
By placing this lying heap of metal down
And embracing his life instead

It's a lot finding a reason to live.

# Amanda Dettmann

### It's a Lot

*prompted by Seema Reza / after Jon Sands*

to ask your father how his day at work was
when he replies, "I think I saw a woman die."

It's a lot to wonder how much cold the postman
can lick through his always open window.

It's a lot to peel an orange slowly
and give a section to your sister.

It's a lot to watch 27 Dresses and wish you were the woman
screaming "Benny and the Jets" on a sticky table
in a bar called Here is Nowhere.

It's a lot to pump gas in 20 degree weather
and think of your friend from New Jersey
who just learned last year.

It's a lot to watch two deer play tag
in front of a moving van.

It's a lot to see an ice grown pond, but no grownups skating.

It's a lot to hug a stranger again
you've met once at a hot chocolate party.

It's a lot to write a Christmas present tag and think,
"Was I funny enough? Will they like what I thought
they would like?"

It's a lot to hold a newborn
and be grateful for not getting pregnant.

It's a lot to see sap blanketing a tree's last sleep.

It's a lot to play inappropriate card games with your mother
when she answers: "balls hanging in my face"

It's a lot to slather olive oil across gnocchi for only half your family.

It's a lot to spin a four-year-old boy with his stuffed bunny in hand
and then leave him for obligations.

It's a lot to hope that when the sun drinks the snow,
the grass outlines an angel. She isn't perfect,

but she's waving in stillness.

# Dilruba Ahmed

## Phase One

For leaving the fridge open
last night, I forgive you.
For conjuring white curtains
instead of living your life.

For the seedlings that wilt, now,
in tiny pots, I forgive you.
For saying no first
but yes as an afterthought.

I forgive you for hideous visions
after childbirth, brought on by loss
of sleep. And when the baby woke
repeatedly, for your silent rebuke

in the dark, "What's your beef?"
I forgive your letting vines
overtake the garden. For fearing
your own propensity to love.

For losing, again, your bag
en route from San Francisco;
for the equally heedless drive back
on the caffeine-fueled return.

I forgive you for leaving
windows open in rain
and soaking library books
again. For putting forth

only revisions of yourself,
with punctuation worked over,
instead of the disordered truth,
I forgive you. For singing mostly

when the shower drowns
your voice. For so admiring
the drummer you failed to hear
the drum. In forgotten tin cans,

may forgiveness gather. Pooling
in gutters. Gushing from pipes.
A great steady rain of olives
from branches, relieved

of cruelty and petty meanness.
With it, a flurry of wings, thirteen
gray pigeons. Ointment reserved
for healers and prophets. I forgive you.

I forgive you. For feeling awkward
and nervous without reason.
For bearing Keats's empty vessel
with such calm you worried

you had, perhaps, no moral
center at all. For treating your mother
with contempt when she deserved
compassion. I forgive you. I forgive

you. I forgive you. For growing
a capacity for love that is great
but matched only, perhaps,
by your loneliness. For being unable

to forgive yourself first so you
could then forgive others and
at last find a way to become
the love that you want in this world.

# Sage Sparrow

## Forgiveness

*prompted by Seema Reza / after Dilruba Ahmed*

Forgiveness is when the wind
moves through the stagnant shape of the basement
where the old cardboard boxes have stacked the dust of clutter
and sweeps it all clean—
just in time
for the flood

Forgiveness rinses as it rises
and its waters wash us clean

In order to forgive myself
I would have to first surrender
my righteous right-handed swinging sword of "I had to do it because..."
and then the left-handed blade that cuts with "What other choice did I have...?"
I would have to look at the shape of my own face in the mirror and say the word

      "Murderer"

Who can forgive someone that kills?
Who forgives someone who murders?

They say in cold blood,
but my blood was warm
It's my body that went cold
It's my body that shook
        that slipped
        that faded

while I waited
while I watched

Forgiveness would require that I admit
Forgiveness would require that I remember
Forgiveness would loosen the wound
        would unravel the tightened tissue of my liver
        would illuminate the radiance of my wrists
                with all their pretty stitches
And say thank you
      thank you

thank you

For a second chance

# Edgar Farr Russell III

## Home to Me Is / Leaving Is

*prompted by Seema Reza / after Dilruba Ahmed*

Home to me is toasting marshmallows, on wire coat hangers, over the fireplace.

Leaving is parents driving me to catch the plane to begin my Air Force career.

Home to me is playing baseball in the alley with younger brother Frazier and neighborhood pals Tommy, Stewart, Petey, and Eddie.

Leaving is walking behind my mother's casket at Arlington National Cemetery.

Home to me is a Memorial Day cookout — Dad by the charcoal grill turning hamburgers; as if behind an altar offering a last Communion with lemonade and potato chips.

Leaving is Frazier and me holding Dad's hand in a Jersey hospital later that same year.

Home to me is binge watching Law & Order with Frazier in his New York apartment.

Leaving is sitting next to Frazier at two funeral services saying goodbye; first to the beloved Alice Anderson; then to her husband Arthur — the real Lucky the Leprechaun.

Home to me is when I will be reunited with those I loved who have gone before.

# Tarfia Faizullah

## What This Elegy Wants

It doesn't want a handful of puffed rice
tossed with mustard oil and chopped chilies,

but wants to understand why a firefly
flares off then on, wants another throatful

or three of whiskey. This elegy is trying
hard to understand how we all become

corpses, but I'm trying to understand
permanence, because this elegy wants

to be the streetlamp above me that darkens
as sudden as a child who, in death, remains

a child. Somewhere, there is a man meant
for me, or maybe just to fall asleep beside me.

Across two oceans, there is a world where
I thought I could live without grief. There,

I watched a vendor reach with hands of lace
towards a woman who looked like me. There,

I fingered bolts of satin I never meant to buy.
There, no one said her name. How to look

into the abyss without leaning forward? How
to gather the morning's flustered shadows

into a river? Tonight, I will watch a man I still
love walk past, hefting another woman's child.

He doesn't look at me. I won't wonder if I
wanted him to. This elegy wonders why

it's so hard to say, I always miss you. Wait,
she might have said. *But didn't you want*

*your palms to be coated in mustard oil? Did you*
*really want to forget the damp scent of my grave?*

# Dartinia Hull

## Cabbage

*prompted by Seema Reza*

On Sunday, I clocked a window.
I whirled around and slammed it with the back of my fist.
My right fist.
The one I'm writing with.
The impact sounded like sex that I kind of remember.
Shock twisted up my arm but I didn't flinch because my husband watched
and he needed to know: *I meant what I meant.*
I impressed myself. Didn't break the glass,
but finger by finger, something delicious Medusa'd through my hair,
massaged my scalp.

That sound, though.

I had to get out.

I turned toward the back door, wild and hungering,
and on the way down the hall,
past the overflowing bookcases *gotta clean these things*
past the table marble, inherited
rammed the same fist into a wall *also didn't break*
that has a thermostat that will talk
and tell you the room
      is too hot
      or too cold
           or too blue
                or too green

or or or.

Call me a liar but this felt
like I'd sunk my teeth into the softest peach
still warm from the roadside stand,
or into the thickest bottom lip.

And then I found a rhythm, tearing through the house,
pushing mail from the bar stools magazines from the counter
and feeling fine about it,
wondering if my hand or my pinky finger was broken

*call the teledoc?*
but this
felt
necessary
like bourbon
           or death
           or books
           or pink
plus, the teledoc costs $45
and I'd rather buy shoes.

On the way to the back door,
I picked up a cabbage from the kitchen counter,
hurled it outside and through the trees,
watched the purple lump roll down the slope,
willed it to slide into the neighbors' yard and settle beside their play set.
Imagined the looks on faces of the little ones.
They'd think it a magical cabbage.

We will not have coleslaw for dinner.

I imagined myself Wonder Woman, hair flying outward,
a burst of electric light, smoke, a gold lasso
that chokes lies;
Or Storm, elemental energy directed to space
that should shatter and crash,
spilling diamonds on the hardwoods,
but didn't so much as crack.

You might thank me.
I'm least trusted when quiet, and still;
then you know I am lighting a match.

I never see myself as Claire
and this week, I am Kamala
smiling, wearing pearls while slicing and ducking and chopping
*insisting*
and shaking my head at an insect

that sniffs out shit better than 47% of the electorate.
I never see myself using the word "electorate."

The cabbage hadn't hurt anyone.
My husband, the feelings I don't admit.
The wall, and window: innocent.

Well.

Sometimes one needs
to salute the absurd
and pull a Bruce Lee on a window.

I have been
letting others pass
insisting that they drive
through my spirit, and throw their trash
out the window.

I am tired of seeing lips move, yet saying nothing that I can comprehend.

My lips included.

That damn lasso.

If you asked what was the matter,
we'd be here until the second coming,
which might be 1000 years after my bones have dissolved,
or might have been yesterday.

It. I'm tired of "it."
All of "it."
A new "it" arises each day. I can't keep up with the its.
They're like stars, galaxies

I'm not inviting you to take my power.
Nor is my power being given as a gift.
Pick any "it."
There's the truth.

In my mind, I am swimming
bathed in salt
perfumed by last night's bourbon
unlined and ungraying

wearing Chuck Taylors and that bikini that had lost the elastic
and slipped off with each barrel wave.
Didn't matter.
It was only breasts and if people hadn't seen breasts, well,
they could consider this their science class.
Pass-fail.

I still wear the Chucks.
Still wear last night's bourbon.

What's left is a bruised hand.
And no cabbage.

# Laura Van Prooyen

## Dark Praise

*prompted by Seema Reza / after Dilruba Ahmed*

My sister had to cut off her breasts. My daughter
asks for a new pancreas. I may be a fool
to believe in goodness. What a risk to love
the soldier who tells me he was hauling ass
when a girl ran in front of his tank. He can't
sleep. I can't sleep. I can't shake the sound
he said her body made. My sister
is a whole new you. She changed her hair,
her name, and she looks good. My daughter
could go blind. We don't talk kidneys
or transplants or amputated feet.
The soldier told me blood is unreal
on a windshield. He can't sleep. He likes
to drink. I like to drink, too. I raise a glass
to my sister's new breasts. Praise my daughter's
needles, insulin, blood tests. I drink for the girl
who, if there's mercy, never knew what was coming.

# Kevin Basl

## Camaraderie

*after Raymond Carver*

[Iraq 2005]


It's July and I have not
had a drink in eight months
except something called Coors
non-alcoholic malt beverage.
Nevertheless, I feel hungover
riding in the Humvee with Doc
and listening to nu metal.
We do not know where we are going,
we are just patrolling.
If I hold my mouth open for too long
my tongue will turn to sandpaper.
Yet, I do not drink water
because my piss bottle is already full
of Doc's snuff spit.
He smiles at me.
At any moment, something could explode.

# Brendan Constantine

## The Needs of the Many

On the days when we wept—
and they were many—we did it
over the sound of a television
or radio, or the many engines
of the sky. It was rarely so quiet
we could hear just our sadness,
the smallness of it
that is merely the sound of wind
and water between the many pages
of the lungs. Many afternoons
we left the house still crying
and drove to a café or the movies,
or back to the hospital where we sat
dumb under the many eyes
of Paul Klee. There were many
umbrellas, days when it refused
to rain, cups of tea ignored. We
washed them all in the sink,
dry eyed. It's been a while,
we're cried out. We collect pauses
and have taken to reading actual
books again. We go through them
like yellow lights, like tunnels
or reunions, we forget which;
the older you are the more similes,
the more pangs per hour. Indeed,
this is how we break one hour into
many, how healing wounds time
in return. And though we know
there will always be crying to do,
just as there's always that song,
always a leaf somewhere in the car,
this may be the only sweetness left,
to have a few griefs we cherish
against the others, which are many.

# Roberta Gomez-Fernandez

## January Six Two Thousand Twenty One

*prompted by Seema Reza / after Kristi Maxwell*

This was after the speech given from Ted Cruz, but before I ate the brown sugared steel cuts.

This was after the feeling of rage had taken over my body, before the discussion about impeachment.

This was after the shock of the confederate flag in the capitol, but before the lame duck trump's address to the American white supremacists.

This was after Maryland admitting it took 1.5 hours to get ahold of the defense secretary for military help clearance, and before the denial that a country's president would retaliate in a way that cost lives.

This was after confusion that we don't have a government that would put such cheapened presidential acts in handcuffs, but before the bold truth pierced through my brain cells and into my amygdala.

This was after the fear that if the capitol building blew up with everyone that represents the American people, but before the thought that I have a president that is a dictator.

This was after the comparison of The Black Lives Matter movement events, but before I rode my bike aimlessly down the bike trail not realizing I was trying to run away from it all.

# Diana Osborn

## Holding and Why

*prompted by Seema Reza / after Megan Alpert*

Fascia of fear hold my fragile parts together as
expectations rest on the vulnerable pelvis bridging the numb
half and the enervated half just where the plain brown sparrow flutters
against rib cage almost smothered by unrelenting lungs
captured in a cartilage corset above the deflated balloon of uterus I take

to bed each night tucked under layers of blubbery pain
beside pearly ovaries within the bloated abdomen
where seeds of velvety contempt ripen. I take

past, present, and future belly to work every week
hopelessly trying to fit it into flat men's clothing to hide
battle wounds of peacetime pleasures of merely eating,
having sex, birthing babies, nursing them into being. I take

silky breasts, bursting with nothing useful anymore to the
abundant grocery store lugging the weighty world of Atlas
in one cup and the bulging boulder of Sisyphus in the
other under a mantle of motherhood grooved shoulders
as I gather my brokenness, and I take

the leg scarred with dangerous dog bites to the vet. I take
creaky weak knees to the oil and lube shop. I take
irritable bowels to the plumbing aisle of Home Depot. I take

private parts to public places and nobody even notices, thank God
and the invisibility cloak of gray hair and thick middle that lets me fly wildly
into windows, and I will walk barefoot through the bloody shards even when I can't
summon saliva or tears or milk.

COMMUNITY BUILDING ART WORKS

# Jennie Clyne

## what she kept

*prompted by Seema Reza / after Megan Alpert*

she kept the sorrow in the small of her back
so that the lightest touch of her lovers embrace
sent a shiver to the top of her skull
she folded it into the tiniest gum wrapper
lost in the bottom of her backpack
stomped flat and pressed into the hem of her pillowcase
filtering in and out of dreams
sometimes waking her so abruptly
in a cold sweat and with a gasp
that she screamed it out loud in the dark
running out in the yard to give it to the man in the moon
she buried it in the yard where the zinnias grow
their sunny faces open with riotous color asking
to be gathered and placed on the dinner table
she baked it into the meatloaf, savory, rich and comforting
reminding her of holidays with grandparents and aunts
from a time when they had not met yet
before she knew
when she stood on the invisible edge of innocence
she collected it in buckets
shells and rusty bolts and bits of sea worn glass
growing heavier and bulkier until she needed a wheelbarrow
and then a dump truck to keep it all contained
then one day she realized she could put it down and walk away.

COMMUNITY BUILDING ART WORKS

# To Everyone in Every Age

*It is a weakening and discoloring idea, that rustic people knew God personally once upon a time—or even knew selflessness or courage or literature—but that it is too late for us. In fact, the absolute is available to everyone in every age. There never was a more holy age than ours, and never a less.*

—Annie Dillard

# Donika Kelly

## Oracle

*prompted by Seema Reza / after Megan Alpert*

The god in my brain
is no god, only a homunculus
I recognize as myself.

The god in my heart,
the same. The god of my liver,
the same. The god

of my guts and thin skin:
me. The homunculus
guiding my father

bears his mustache
and heavy-lidded eyes.
Was it he who placed

the god in me that is me?
And what do I mean
by God, I wonder.

I take my questions
to the oracle, another
homunculus, and I say either:

*Who placed the god in me?*
*What do I mean, when I say god?*

The reply to either
being, *Your father.*

*Stupid oracle*, I think,
fathers are for children,

and I was never a child,
only a smaller image of myself.

# Diane Neff

## Time

*prompted by Seema Reza / after Stephen Dunn*

Rare, that love that feels the same in the morning and the evening,

when your habit of greeting each interruption as a possibility

brings a smile to my brain while I groan aloud, my thoughts broken.

Who are you, to welcome the world in, to embrace the unplanned?

I need my color-coded, half-hour schedule to survive, and yet

I do, and move on, and settle, just to have my day shattered

again, and then mended with steel and silk threads

woven, tempered, and smoothed by your peace.

The steady tick of your father's mantel clock marks heartbeats –

those we only remember, and those that will continue

because you remember to wind the key each Tuesday.

# Cyrus Sepahbodi

## To All the Men I've Loved Before

*prompted by Hari Alluri / for Arthur Kayzakian*

A piece of furniture and my first pair
of cherry-red, black-and-white striped
Air Jordan's is all I remember of the year
Ahmad Ali Baharlou died.

When I wore those sneakers, my feet were
Saturn V rockets and I had mad hops,
speed like MJ.

Tap the rim during gym class?
    *Easy.*
Grab all the boards at recess?
    *Cake.*
Catch the kid that jumped me
during 4th period computer class?
    *No problem.*

Move from home,
drop friendless into Portolla MS
3200 kids that want to beat my ass,
three families piled together
sharing bedrooms with cousins,
aunts, uncles, grandparents
in a blue house off Nogales drive
with so much dark inside of it?
    *WATCH ME.*

But there is no jumping over lung cancer,
or how the body is a construction of ghosts,
a dirty highway, a rusty swing-set,
and the poor facsimile of
what it means to be a man—
there is no roadmap for being 6 years old
and having abandonment issues.

So, tell me what my fists are saying.
Teach me how the mouth is a failed apology,
a mosque made from rusted canary wings
built by a little boy with beautiful hair,

little fingers clasped at the shirt tail of his namesake,
this is how we pray, 5 times per day,
the little blue book pointing us to Mecca—
*allahu akbar hafezeh uh hafezeh, Alhamdallah.*

I ask god if life is sacred how can the dinner
we ate last night turn to dust in his lungs.
This is how to learn that cancer eats alveoli
like stale theater popcorn or moths to a
starch-pressed wedding tuxedo
hanging in my father's closet.

And that damn cream-colored couch that we lugged
3000 miles in July heat, my palpable excitement
for a new school furled into regret from a busted lip
by the basketball courts. I may have been born with
two tongues but my skin speaks only one.

There is a phrase in my father's tongue
for when a 12-year-old boy watches an old man die.
The river of quiet seeping from his face.
Pants tied around chemo-starved waistlines sponged
into leather couches trying to stay awake.

The word is *Kaleh Malag* and it means somersault.
I am 34 now still learning to pronounce the word love.
Or little bird. Dervishing around my axis
I still tie my laces too tight, think of spaceflight
pulse oxygen readouts, born into a family
with sweaty palms
searching for a father
in every man I meet.

# Carla Rachel Sameth

## [I am a woman of almost 62 years old,]

*prompted by Seema Reza / after Mary Oliver*

I am a woman of almost 62 years old,
of no special bravery.
Everyday, I wake up to my wife
clutching me tightly, then singing loudly,
the cat, once a teen mama, pounding on the door,
last night's gunshots not yet forgotten.
Turn up the sound I say,
that song about waking up and working hard each day
though I am a woman inert, until I decide
to throw off all the weighted memories:
loud red-faced baboons,
falling down interiors, the magic elastic
that holds my unkind body
tight to my imagination
until I step out and blow kisses
to the hummingbird, frantic, ecstatic,
or just doing its job,
circling the Bird of Paradise.

I am two years older
than the 60th birthday party
my son, my friends, my family threw for me
the trio playing songs I'd once danced to:
with baby in sling, Ojos Negros, Piel Canela
the carne, the aguas, las flores,
pastel de las tres leches,
my friend Gary showing up
only to jump from a parking structure weeks later.
He told me, it's been a rough year
and I agreed, it's been a year
and he said, we'll talk.
But we never did, not really.
He only called me to tell me how proud
he is of me, my son, all we've done.
And damn him, he didn't wait for that conversation
about the obliterating fog, the deep downward slide,
the gray gray as if he were another Seattle child,
or whatever said to him,
Jump Gary, jump.

I am a woman almost 62
who once had moxie, chopped wood,
built trails, leaped in front of skinheads
who threatened me and my two sisters.
I am a tiny speck lost in a corner
wondering if I'll rise up and blow out to the sky
when we finally can open the doors.
I am a forgotten thought that bore a hole
through skull from too much pounding.
I am still the nail
that may not always bend,
the mango that is sweet and spicy,
chile and limon that brings your mouth alive.
I am the lips that remember the softest kisses
billowing across continents
only to discover they were once here,
right beside me.
I am the skater leaping,
flying, shimmying a fountain
of joy and since I'm not,
my son is. Sliding through Venice Beach
and home again to me.
I am the arms that held my young son,
milky sweet sweat, then opened up
skyward watching him soar.

# Erik Schwab

## Arrival

*prompted by Seema Reza / after Mary Oliver*

I am a man of fifty-three years old, of no special
shock value to the 23-year-old or the 83-year-old
in this sci-fi movie where all times happen at once
and trot up to meet each other like square dancers,
or at the office where time is just one thing after another.

In today's scene, the time is frenzied, everything is going wrong,
I am played by Buster Keaton, stone-faced, bailing out a rowboat,
the house whirling on its foundation in the dust, the steam train barreling down.
This glorious chaos, the bridge collapsing under the train, this
release from order and obligation, it feels so good
when you're sitting in the theater in the dark. It feels like
a good cry. Your ribs are there. Your throat, your heated face.
But what about our hero? Yes, I know he's fiction. I am not fiction.
I'm shoveling coal into the train's hungry furnace and pulling the whistle.
Bushes and crabgrass blur into soup. No one can possibly live
at such speeds. There will be bloodstains and flattened pennies all over the place.
There will be snare drums and elephant ears but the carnival somehow
never starts, a breakfast of anticipation and a riot of screaming goats
somewhere outside the house. It was years ago but it is always time to feed them
every tin can the miners threw away, every museum piece, every
Campbell's soup, each Marilyn nostalgic for her future.

Every day I wind the clock. It ticks down rubato, slow then quick
like a sleeping lion, contemptuous of calendars. The goats scream
and jump into the trees. Sure, let's call me fifty-three again. This prime number
thinks it's so goddamn special just because it's awake, just because it's my turn
to buzz back at a few cicadas, to play a bandoneon or throw it in the swamp.
To wash my face whether the sun is out or not.

# Preeti Kaur Dhaliwal

## lullabied fraction

*prompted by Seema Reza / after Mary Oliver*

I am a woman of 34 years old no longer
misplacing her love in the body

of pain

before pleasure, grazing her cheek
against moss rather than the face of

a lover

inking the ocean on her ribcage
to stop her body from swelling

with extraction blooming

a lotus from her limbs to lend
her lullabied fraction of a story

compounding

within her, waltzing a past she cannot reach
nips at her toes

she pens

the divine onto her foot
a word her people have forgotten

it used to be easy

for her to lodge loss
between the skin of her and another

now a woman

of 34 years, untouched
cognizance waves across her chest, flowers

from my ribs

shakti, her step collecting fallen leaves
as I learn long division—

try to make a whole.

# Seema Yasmin

## Disease Is Not the Only Thing That Spreads

What else is contagious: Ellen's long tongue.
A rumor we buried daddy in an unmarked
grave. History. Pathogens criss-crossing agar
-plated petri dishes like rebel soldiers breaching
trenches. This story: that we had it coming,
that we are good only for uncivil wars and dis
-eases. That we prayed for colonization. Blood.
Microbes escaping test tubes conquering
lab countertops slower than hearsay, she say
we burned Daddy's corpse like bad Muslims;
like White (coated) doctors instructed. What else
is contagious: doctored death certificates. Half
-truths. Cursive. Ink. They say there is no cure
then there is a cure only for them. So. What
else spreads: knots of grief twisting bowels
into distended loops of fermenting torment. No
days of mourning. Two years of outside
intervention. Armies. Conviction. Belief that
this will spread & spread. That all contagions
wax endemic. This one will never     end.

# Anne Barlieb

## A Pilgrimage of Many Truths[1]

*Prompted by Seema Reza / After listening to "Build, Now, a Monument" by
Matthew Olzmann and being prompted to pay attention to what I'm
paying attention to, a 20-minute write, and, my God—that hourglass, a
staircase, the overturned vehicle[2] and this caterpillar...*

My mother is making a pilgrimage through the house
And around my father now confined to a hospital bed
In what used to be "the back room", the-living-room-
-turned-dying-room all in one breath, at once
I can imagine the TV bolted to the panel wall
Making noise about current events: vaccines
and Rush Limbaugh dead from lung cancer,
Not at all relevant to or registering in what is left of my father's life now
As a morphine bag hangs suspended
Waiting and not waiting
Morphine doesn't know of waiting

My mother's handwriting changed in the last few years
And the last few months, especially
The cards she sends are like mile markers along a declining road that feels like it could
        get steep around the next corner or two
Children are forced uphill as parents travel downhill,
Atop, we find the water stain of a tide that's risen and been washed back out to sea, the
        height an exact match to that of the witness and is perfectly level

I ask her how she is doing
*Your father is fading away*, she tells me
I lean into the silence
*We are drinking a lot of orange juice*
I lean further into the silence
Your father's been very thirsty, wakes me up a few times in the night wanting a drink. I
        don't mind it
Leaning further
I'll have to go get more of the juice because we're almost out

I lean, still further, thinking my mother is 80 years old today

---

1  excerpted from "A Writing Group, The Great Work, and Other Acts of God"
2  imagery from Olzmann's poem and my own suicide attempt in January 2015

And I am nearly the age my parents were when they adopted me, forty years ago
I'm tired,
Silence turned hesitation, I'm not sure if hers or mine
But we all get tired, don't we, isn't that normal?
As if asking this question to herself, she sighs an exasperated sigh as if to answer her
      own question

You don't have to be the strong one, my therapist told me, her voice in my head now
      because, like morphine,
Mercy doesn't know of waiting
Your mother is losing her husband and it must be hard
This is true, of course
and there are many truths revealed in total losses like death
I hang up
And cry long and hard, as we do in these great pilgrimages, bent over, my head
      in my hands—
Because I'm losing the father I had
and who he was
Because I'm losing the father I didn't have
and who he wasn't
Because of the mother I have
Because of the mother I have not[3]

Because of everything this is right now and all that it isn't
Because of who I am
Because of who I haven't been
Because of who I have yet to become (if ever)
Because this is change & I have no choice but to adapt along with it
Because who among us doesn't have life-altering, crippling adverse childhood
      experiences sometime during the course of our lives?
Because long journeys, traveled slowly, still turn so quickly to who-knows-where and
      feeling the loss or injustice of many truths makes pilgrims of us all

---

[3] *In memory of my birth mother, Brenda Blodwyn Bellon Calder Telford – March 4, 1996*

# Aissatou Sunjata

## Rumination

*prompted by Seema Reza / after Matthew Olzmann*

There are times sitting here
on red flannel sheets
an eye flutter from dreams
sequestered from the outside world
by choice, age and medical ailments
I long to shave off some years
like the street vendor remembered in youth
yelling for children and their money to join him
he scraped blocks of ice into paper cone-shaped cups
what flavor syrup he would ask
pour a sweet rainbow choice over crushed ice
while seeing how much more money
by heads and in pockets behind a temporary leader.
Want to return to a time when even I questioned my existence
whether cells and an egg met by mistake to form me
perhaps I was supposed to be something else.
A firefly declaring presence by lighting the way
maybe a butterfly transforming itself before stillness
or a dragonfly skimming over shimmering ripples
with minimum effort knowing its life cycle brief
it must live in the moment/embrace it all
its natural evolution
death looms at its birth
in-between fancy its life of purpose
and gaiety in the same dance
want to be that being
one who dances in the face of inevitability
instead of wearing age like a well-worn housecoat
whose still functioning snaps secure with firmness
though now its rose-print faded by time, washing and wear
I want to become it before it faced old age
when it was new crisp and its snaps shiny.
When it had not yet formed to a body's silhouette
promised what it would never truly provide for long
warmth, security against exposure to harshness
it will not last, in time begins to wear thin
return to being tattered fabric
I want my ending to become something more
than simply death

let it become a beginning/rebirth
my soul sometimes imagines impossibility
another few years left of life
let me live my life again
before gray hair and weary limbs
wrinkles permanently etched on my flesh
were signs of my life and many unkempt promises
not even a wave of God's wand can alter.

# Howard S. Carman, Jr.

## Magical Workshop

*prompted by Shuly Xóchitl Cawood / after José Olivarez*

The first poem I ever kept is not very good—
unimaginative and homogeneous. I kept it anyway.
Those words captured, even poorly, a spectacular
summertime walk in Northumberland.
That poem became part of my being
and still reflects who I was when I wrote it.

Today, I met new poets—
new to me, at least—
in a Zoom workshop.
Not homogeneous at all,
they were diverse, vivid in color and sound,
like words of a good poem.

Without leaving my office,
I entered a magical forest
of bipedal trees, rooted in language:
ebony, mahogany, pine, ash, and birch
with leaves of blonde, brunette, auburn, gray,
even purple.

Gemstones reflected sunlight—
and love—
with tints of brown, hazel, blue, green,
and amber. Birds sang with accents
of Farsi, Hindi, Sioux, Ukrainian,
even American English.

The trees spoke words
that thundered in my ears,
thumped on my chest,
rained on my cheeks,
and changed who I was
into who I am.

Too soon, a mouse scampered across my desk
and everything disappeared into black.
But the forest poets now live in this poem
and are forever part of my being,

like that first poem.
I think I will keep this one, too.

# Brionne Janae

## child's pose

*prompted by Shuly Xóchitl Cawood / after José Olivarez*

imagine your heart is just a ball you learned to dribble up
and down the length of your driveway back home. slow down

control it. plant your feet in the soft blue of your mat and release
it is hard but slowly you are unlearning the shallow pant

of your childhood. extend your body—do not reach
for someone but something fixed and fleshless and certain—

fold flatten then lift your head like a cobra sure of the sun
waiting and ready to caress the chill

from its scales. inhale—try not to remember how desperate
you've been for touch—yes ignore it—that hitch of your heart

you got from mornings you woke to find momma hysterical
or gone. try to give up the certainty she'd never return

recall only the return and not its coldness. imagine her arms
wide to receive you imagine you are not a thing that needs

escaping. it is hard and though at times you are sure
you will always be the abandoned girl trying to abandon herself

push up arch deep into your back inhale and remember—
when it is too late to pray the end of the flood

we pray instead to survive it.

# Garrett Bryant

## [Denver, March-July 2020]

*prompted by Hari Alluri, Brandon Constantine, Faisal Mohyuddin, Seema Reza*
*gratitude*

I.

Safety is a question of breath as I walk
over to a neighbor's house, a fresh loaf of sourdough tucked
under my arm. With a single knuckle, I knock—the door
rattles, slightly ajar, and I quickly tiptoe backward to a
distance defined as *safe*. A single knuckle pushes the door
open, but only a few inches. Softly, my tongue
unzips an offering, and my palms lay the bread to
ground. I've never heard a more throated *thank you*, as I turn
home to safety, or solitude, waiting for the bread to rest between folds.

II.

*[...] because in times like these*
*to have you listen at all, it's necessary*
*to talk about trees.*
> —Adrienne Rich, "What Kind of Times Are These" (Dark Fields of
> the Republic: Poems 1991-1995)

Dear,

I'm writing to tell you that for the first time in my life, I've dusted the top of my
refrigerator—
so strange, the settled pieces of us, sticky with grease and steam
blooms from an oven well-used.

I've noticed, also, how dust collects in the window sills—tiny dunes in the corners,
huddled in prayer.

The trees outside the windows are still.

Dear, you wouldn't believe the things I've discovered—the Spring
inside my home, awakening under quarantine—and in the eyes of a lover,
a new language, familiar, yet I can't place it.

There's music in the way we dance around each other in the hallway.

And I must tell you, Dear, I smell earth in the sofa.

When the music of a city is shuttered in quarantine,
a field mouse can be heard shuffling in the leaves
for spring shoots of sweet-pea, fallen crabapple blossoms.
There's prayer to this scuttle.

As there is prayer in the new rituals cooling our breath.

It's Tuesday, Dear, and another black man has been killed by police—
knees pressed into his neck as if trying to put the man back into the earth.

But the earth has been full for too long, so I hold this ritual in my body—it carries me
through the mornings, as I remember names to the trees outside—

Breonna, George, Elija, Ahmaud.

Dear, I'm writing to tell you that it's ok to sit with the silence of a morning.

I'm writing to tell you that it's ok to let fear crack in your throat.

It's ok to just listen, Dear, to bacon frying in the neighbor's kitchen, to spring
grass pulling up the soil.

Listen for the trees whispering in each other's hearts—the soft beats
between beats—trees we must keep naming like our own reflections
cupped in the water of two palms.

Listen for the language of snow, for the dream in waiting, for dough to rest between
folds.

# Gowri Koneswaran

## A Year of Collective Isolation

*prompted by Seema Reza*

This heavy humid between us.
Squinting at sunlight on window.

The tops of trees, parched.
My eyelids, flaking and splintered.

When I'm afraid, my throat.
Open palms mark my brave.

Rainworks explode on the roof.
The rush and storm invited.

One hour: inches of rain.
A flooded road reads reverse.

We ascend the city's hills,
seek and find safe moment.

Family nearby? No. The rules,
revised and revised. Such daily

talk of masks. Our mouths,
our empty swallow. This absence

harder to feed. In grief,
a distant wake streams mourning.

So many condolences, no hugs.
Our arms apart, we carry.

# Afterword
## by Seema Reza

### We Were Not Alone

In 2001, I was a high-school-dropout-part-time-community-college-student-young-mother with no organizational or institutional affiliation. No authority, no "in." The day after 9/11, overcome by grief and panic, and moved by an urgency I had never known, I organized an interfaith vigil in my city's square. I called houses of worship from the phone book and invited clergy and congregations. I put an ad in the local paper. I'd never done anything like it before. Nearly everyone I encountered helped me. I called City Hall to ask about a permit and the person on the other end of the line waved me along. "You'll be fine," she said. I didn't know if anyone outside of my family would show up. But on the evening of Friday, September 14th, they did. People came from far away looking for us, others happened to be passing and stopped quietly to join. I don't know if I said anything, I know I didn't have something to say, that wasn't the point. We sat in the darkening grass and lit candles. The dark deepened. We passed more candles. We all needed the same thing, and we couldn't get it alone.

Nine years later, I answered an ad for a job teaching art at Walter Reed Army Medical Center. I have no military experience, no one in my family had ever served. Our country was at war with Muslims, and both Islamophobic hate crimes and profiling and surveillance of Muslims had spiked in the past few years. I had no reason to feel like I belonged.

Within a few months of taking that job, my marriage came to an end, my father drowned in the ocean, my grandfather succumbed to his dementia, a beloved uncle died after a long, ravaging illness. My grief, so bare and isolating in a world of positive psychology "choose your attitude" pep talks, might have sunk me, but at Walter Reed I was surrounded by people whose grief was also undeniable. They wore it—on their faces, in their posture, under their bandages, and sometimes in their anger. We made art, shared poetry and difficult stories. We laughed and laughed and laughed. What we all needed was a place to bring both our pain and our joy. What we all needed was space to stop denying our grief so we could finally expand beyond it, to be more than, as Jon Sands writes, "a caricature of our griefs." One folding table became two, then three, then four. People pulled up chairs, invited more people. Along the way, people helped create this space. A decade has passed.

For the past year and a half, the world has been frozen by the COVID-19 pandemic. During the first week of lockdown, we moved our workshops at Walter Reed and Fort Belvoir online and opened them to everyone, regardless of military connection. I wasn't certain anyone would come. But they did. Thousands of people, from all over the world.

As I sit to write this, the 20th anniversary of 9/11 approaches. Last summer, the murders of George Floyd and Breonna Taylor brought protests to cities all over the country. Earlier this year, we watched an angry mob overrun the US Capitol. Wildfires burn, the smoke spreads across the Western sky. Somewhere, always, something is burning. Last week, the Taliban took cities across Afghanistan as US troops were withdrawn. Thirteen US Service Members died. We don't have a clear count of how many Afghans were killed. We grieve. Each week there are new reasons to grieve. And we live. We make more and more space. Annie Dillard writes: "There was never a more holy age than ours, and never a less."

The darkness deepens, and we pass more candles. And all along the way, people help. By buying this book, you are helping. By reading these honest accounts, by writing your own, you are passing a candle. We are not alone.

# Notes & Acknowledgements

**Dilruba Ahmed** is the author of *Bring Now the Angels* (Pitt Poetry Series, 2020), with poems featured in *New York Times Magazine*, *Best American Poetry 2019*, and podcasts such as *The Slowdown* with Tracy K. Smith and *Poetry Unbound* with Pádraig Ó Tuama. Her debut book of poetry, *Dhaka Dust* (Graywolf Press, 2011), won the Bakeless Prize. Ahmed's poems have appeared in *Kenyon Review*, *New England Review*, and *Ploughshares*, and are widely anthologized. Ahmed is the recipient of The Florida Review's Editors' Award, a Dorothy Sargent Rosenberg Memorial Prize, and the Katharine Bakeless Nason Fellowship in Poetry awarded by the Bread Loaf Writers Conference. www.dilrubaahmed.com

> "Phase One" is from *Bring Now the Angels* by Dilruba Ahmed © 2020. Reprinted by permission of the University of Pittsburgh Press.

**Hari Alluri** is the author of *The Flayed City* (Kaya). A winner of the 2020 Leonard A. Slade, Jr. Poetry Fellowship and recipient of grants from the BC Arts Council and Canada Council for the arts, his work appears widely in anthologies, journals, and online venues, including *Apogee*, *Asian American Literary Review*, *Poetry*, *Split This Rock*, *Witness*, and elsewhere.

> "Blessing Wednesday (Cousin of Rattan)" is after the "Pinsan ng Rattan" card in Jana Lynne Umipig's *Kapwa Tarot* and is originally published in *Capitalism Nature Socialism*, reprinted here by permission of the author.

**Anthony Almojera** was born and raised in Brooklyn NY in 1977. He lived most of my life there with the exception of short stints in Bozeman Montana and Los Angeles. He has travelled to 90 countries and territories and currently works for the FDNY as a paramedic lieutenant. He has been working there for 18 years and was front and center for the brunt of the pandemic in NYC.

> "13 bodies [a day in the life of a pandemic paramedic]" is prompted by Seema Reza.

**Anne Barlieb** medically retired from the Army after 14 years of service, in 2018. Her writing can be found in hand written journals, a few select writing group anthologies, and volumes of personal email traffic with fellow inbox hitch-hikers. Always a pen in one hand, thumb out with the other.

> "A Pilgrimage of Many Truths" is after Matthew Olzmann's "Build, Now, a Monument," prompted by Seema Reza on February 19, 2021; this piece is the third part of a longer poem entitled "A Writing Group, The Great Work, and Other Acts of God."

**Kevin Basl** is a writer and musician living near Ithaca, New York. He served in the U.S. Army, twice deploying to Iraq. He holds an MFA from Temple University, where he has taught writing. Since 2013, he has facilitated numerous art and writing workshops for service members, veterans and their communities.

> "Camaraderie" is after Raymond Carver, prompted by Seema Reza.

**Mahogany L. Browne** is a writer, organizer & educator. Executive Director of Bowery Poetry Club & Artistic Director of Urban Word NYC & Poetry Coordinator at St. Francis College. Browne has received fellowships from Agnes Gund, Air Serenbe, Cave Canem, Poets House, Mellon Research & Rauschenberg. She is the author of recent works: *Chlorine Sky*, *Woke: A Young Poets Call to Justice*, *Woke Baby*, & *Black Girl Magic*. As the founder of the diverse lit initiative, Woke Baby Book Fair, Browne is excited to release her newest poetry collection responding to the impact of mass incarceration on women and children: *I Remember Death By Its Proximity to What I Love* (Haymarket Books). She lives in Brooklyn, NY.

"Redbone Dances" is originally published in *Redbone*, copyright © 2015 by Mahogany Browne and reprinted here by permission of the author and Willow Books.

**Garrett Bryant** is a poet, artist, editor and teacher from Alpine, California—Kumeyaay land. He currently lives and writes from a converted school bus tiny home with his partner Blue. He has been a contributing editor for Poetry International, and is the co-founder of Poetic Youth, a community outreach and creative writing program serving underserved youth. Garrett's work can be found in *Harpur Palate*, *Faultline*, *The Winnow*, *Cordite Poetry Review*, *Southword Journal* and *Helen*, among others.

"[Denver, March-July 2020]" was written in multiple CBAW workshops, prompted by Hari Alluri, Brandon Constantine, Faisal Mohyuddin, and Seema Reza—gratitude.

**Howard S. Carman, Jr.**, Ph.D., is a retired research chemist living in East Tennessee with his wife, Karen. His poetry has won awards from the National Federation of State Poetry Societies and the Poetry Society of Tennessee, for which he serves as Treasurer and Membership Chair of the Northeast Chapter.

"Magical Workshop" is after José Olivarez's "Ode to the First White Girl I Ever Loved," prompted by Shuly Xóchitl Cawood on August 7, 2020.

**Shuly Xóchitl Cawood**'s poetry collection, *Trouble Can Be So Beautiful at the Beginning* (Mercer University Press) won the Adrienne Bond Award for Poetry. Cawood's other books include *A Small Thing to Want: stories* (Press 53) and the memoir, *The Going and Goodbye* (Platypus Press). Learn more at www.shulycawood.com.

"Letter to the Children of the Future" is prompted by Caryn Mirriam-Goldberg on September 30, 2020.

**Ruth Christopher** is a poet, dancer, intersectional feminist, mixed media artist, and sometimes musician. She is a senior at Davis where she is an Osher Honors scholar writing her thesis on Sylvia Plath's poetry. She is a co-founder of the organization Mad Mouth Poetry which you can check out at madmouthpoetry.com.

"On Tuesdays We Go to Senator Jones" is after Faisal Mohyuddin's "Ghazal for the Diaspora," prompted by Hari Alluri on August 19, 2020.

**Jennie Clyne** is an ER nurse working in San Francisco. Jennie enjoys creative expression through photography, music, painting, and fiber arts, using them as a means to slow down and appreciate small gestures and the ordinary moment. She turned to writing poetry as a way to process the stress of working through the pandemic on the front lines.

"What She Kept" is after Megan Alpert's "What We Kept," prompted by Seema Reza on January 12, 2021.

**Brendan Constantine** is a poet based in Los Angeles. His work has appeared in many of the nation's standards, including *Best American Poetry*, *Tin House*, *Ploughshares*, *Prairie Schooner*, and *Poem-a-Day*. His most recent collections are *Dementia, My Darling* (2016) from Red Hen Press and *Bouncy Bounce* (2018) a chapbook from Blue Horse Press. New work is forthcoming in *Poetry* and *The Hope in the Head Review*. He has received support and commissions from the Getty Museum, James Irvine Foundation, and the National Endowment for the Arts. www.brendanconstantine.com

"The Needs of the Many" is originally published in *Poem-a-Day* on November 13, 2015, by the Academy of American Poets, reprinted here by permission of the author.

**Rachelle Cruz** is the author of a poetry collection, *God's Will for Monsters*; a comics textbook and resource, *Experiencing Comics: An Introduction to Reading, Discussing and Creating Comics*; an anthology of Philippine mythology with Lis P. Sipin-Gabon, *Kuwento: Lost Things*.

"The You" is after Steven Universe's *Lion* / after reading a fragment of Toni Morrison's *Jazz*, prompted by Hari Alluri.

**Kim Defiori** served in the Army as a Military Police Officer. After several traumatic events, she struggled with the effects of Post Traumatic Stress Disorder (PTSD) and Traumatic Brain Injuries (TBI). Kim sought treatment after several suicide attempts. She's a graduate of West Point and obtained her MBA from Cornell University.

"Reasons to Live" is after Jon Sands's "It's a Lot," prompted by Seema Reza on December 18, 2020.

**Amanda Dettmann** is a poet whose current work explores womanhood, eating disorders, existence, and becoming. Her work can be found in her poetry book *Untranslatable Honeyed Bruises* as well as the following literary journals: *Underwood Press: Black Works* (Dark Imagery Issue), *The Mosaic*, *Angles*, and *The National Poetry Quarterly*.

"It's a Lot" is after Jon Sands's "It's a Lot," prompted by Seema Reza on December 18, 2020.

**Preeti Kaur Dhaliwal** (she/her) is a Punjabi critical race feminist, writer, lawyer, college prof and facilitator who grew up on unceded Coast Salish territories. She recently completed her first novel manuscript in the University of Guelph's MFA program. When she's not editing, writing or marking, she's likely playing with collage or visiting moss, ocean and trees.

"lullabied fraction" is after Mary Oliver's "Work," prompted by Seema Reza on February 5, 2021.

**Tarfia Faizullah** was born in Brooklyn, New York, and raised in Texas. She is the author of *Registers of Illuminated Villages* (Graywolf Press, 2018) and *Seam* (Southern Illinois University Press, 2014). She lives in Dallas, Texas. Tarfia's writing appears widely in the U.S.

and abroad in the *Daily Star*, *Hindu Business Line*, *BuzzFeed*, *PBS News Hour*, *Huffington Post*, *Poetry Magazine*, *Ms. Magazine*, the Academy of American Poets' *Poem-a-Day*, *Oxford American*, the *New Republic*, the *Nation*, *Halal If You Hear Me* (Haymarket, 2019), and has been displayed at the Smithsonian, the Rubin Museum of Art, and elsewhere.

"What This Elegy Wants" is originally published in *Registers of Illuminated Villages*, copyright © 2015 by Tarfia Faizullah, reprinted here by permission of the author and Willow Books.

**Tiffany Nicole Fletcher** is a writer and vocalist whose poems focus on spirituality, nature, and empowerment. A first-generation West Indian-American, she was raised in New York City.

"One Thing I Know" is after Leah Horlick's "Liberation," prompted by Jennifer Patterson in her Virtual Writing + Breathwork Workshop on June 19, 2020.

**Ross Gay** is the author of four books of poetry: *Against Which*; *Bringing the Shovel Down*; *Be Holding*; and *Catalog of Unabashed Gratitude*, winner of the 2015 National Book Critics Circle Award and the 2016 Kingsley Tufts Poetry Award. His new poem, *Be Holding*, was released from the University of Pittsburgh Press in September of 2020. His collection of essays, *The Book of Delights*, was released by Algonquin Books in 2019.

"ode to the puritan in me" is originally published in *Catalog of Unabashed Gratitude*, copyright © 2015 by Ross Gay, reprinted by permission of University of Pittsburgh Press.

**Aracelis Girmay** is the author of the poetry collections *Teeth*, *Kingdom Animalia*, and *the black maria*. She is also the author/collagist of the picture book *changing, changing*, and with her sister collaborated on the recently published *What Do You Know?* Girmay is on the editorial board of the African Poetry Book Fund and recently curated *How to Carry Water: Selected Poems of Lucille Clifton*.

"Elegy" is originally published in *Kingdom Animalia*, copyright © 2011 by Aracelis Girmay, reprinted here by permission of the author and BOA Editions, Ltd.

**Roberta Gomez-Fernandez** is a psychotherapist, consultant, and writer based out of Los Angeles, California. She is the founder of A Space to Pause, which provides therapy and consultation to individuals and organizations seeking to improve their work spaces. This poem is her first publication.

"This Was After... " is after Kristi Maxwell's "After After," prompted by Seema Reza on December 30, 2020.

**Joan Smith Green** is a wife, mom, gramma, and retired educator. She is a determined survivor; earned a black belt in Kempo Karate; and has learned to enjoy life and its challenges. Participating in CBAW.org workshops has helped Joan rediscover and nurture her love of creative expression by combining her positive outlook with words and art.

"Ain't Nothin' But A Thang" is prompted by Amelia Bane.

**Hannah Grieco** is a writer and editor in Arlington, VA. Her work can be found in a wide variety of publications, both literary and freelance. She is the cnf editor at JMWW, the fiction editor at Porcupine Literary, and the founder and organizer of the monthly reading series 'Readings on the Pike' in the DC area. Find her online at www.hgrieco.com and on Twitter @writesloud.

"Release Valve" is originally published in *Entropy* on February 9, 2021, reprinted here by permission of the author.

**Elizabeth Hassler** (she/her) is a poet, organizer, and service-user who organizes around disabled art and writes about being and longing. Her work explores dimensions of her life in all its privilege, femmeness, disability and play from Arcata, CA, also known as Wiyot land.

"Krill" is after Faisal Mohyuddin's "Ghazal for the Diaspora," prompted by Hari Alluri on August 19, 2020.

**Raychelle Heath** is a poet, artist, teacher, podcaster, BIPOC writing party facilitator, and digital nomad with an MFA in Writing. She is also an alumni of the Voices of Our Nations Arts Foundation workshop. Her work has been published in *Alimentum Magazine* and in *Travel Noire*.

"If We Could Once Upon a Time" is after Yusef Komunyakaa's "Thanks," prompted by Joe Merritt on August 26, 2020.

**Nicole Arocho Hernández** is a poet from Cabo Rojo, Puerto Rico. Her poems have appeared in *Variant Literature Journal* and *The Acentos Review*, among others. Her first chapbook, *I Have No Ocean*, was published by Sundress Publications. She is an MFA Candidate at Arizona State University. Find her on social media: @nimaarhe

"asked to write about my muse— | [muscle]" is prompted by Yesenia Montilla on September 23, 2020.

**Dartinia Hull** has been published in *iPondr*, *The Bitter Southerner*, *MUTHA Magazine*, *Noteworthy*, and *CNN*. She's a graduate of the Queen's University of Charlotte Master of Fine Arts program. Her essay "The Room With the Dying Fan" was a reader favorite in *The Bitter Southerner*'s 2019 Folklore Project.

"Cabbage" is prompted by Seema Reza.

**Joy Jacobson** is a poet and medical editor in New York.

"Praise: A Cento" is after Joy Harjo's "Praise the Rain," gathered from the CBAW Crew's affirmation chat on September 9, 2020.

**Brionne Janae** is a poet and teaching artist living in Brooklyn. They are the author of *Blessed are the Peacemakers* (2021) which won the 2020 Cave Canem Northwestern University Press Poetry Prize, and *After Jubilee* (2017) published by Boat Press. Brionne has received fellowships to Cave Canem, Sewanee Writers Conference, Vermont Studio Center and Hedgebrook. Their poetry has been published in *Ploughshares*, *The American Poetry Review*, The Academy of American Poets' *Poem-a-Day*, *The Sun Magazine*, *jubilat*, and *Waxwing*, among others. Off the page they go by Breezy.

"Child's Pose" is originally published in *Poem-a-Day* on August 22, 2018, by the Academy of American Poets, reprinted here by permission of the author.

The wife of a retired Marine, **Brenda Johnson** retired from the DOD school system at Camp Lejeune, NC. She wrote poems as examples for her students. After retiring she joined a consortium of local poets. She attended poetry workshops sponsored by the local arts council and submitted a few for publication.

"We Were Never Taught Anything About Love Except "Jesus Loves Me"" is after Shin Ji Moon's "Kintsugi," prompted by Seema Reza.

**Arthur Kayzakian** is a poet, editor and educator. His chapbook, *My Burning City*, was a finalist for the Locked Horn Press Chapbook Prize and Two Sylvias Press Chapbook Prize. His poems and translations have appeared in several publications including *Taos Journal of International Poetry & Art*, and *Prairie Schooner*.

"Translation" is prompted by Hari Alluri, with nods to the CBAW brainstorm: images and lines shared by participants on May 22, 2020. The poem is originally published in *Nat. Brut*, reprinted here by permission of the author.

**Donika Kelly** is the author of *Bestiary*, winner of the 2015 Cave Canem Poetry Prize, the 2017 Hurston/Wright Award for poetry, and the 2018 Kate Tufts Discovery Award. Her most recent collection is *The Renunciations* (Graywolf). A Cave Canem graduate fellow and member of the collective Poets at the End of the World, Donika has also received a Lannan Residency Fellowship, and a summer workshop fellowship from the Fine Arts Work Center. Her poems have been published in *The New Yorker*, *The Atlantic* online, *The Paris Review*, and *Foglifter*.

"Oracle" is originally published in *Black Warrior Review* in 2018, retrieved from *Verse Daily*, reprinted here by permission of the author.

**Gowri Koneswaran** is a queer Tamil writer, performing artist, teacher, and lawyer. Her work has been published in the *Journal of Asian American Studies*, *Environmental Health Perspectives*, *Adi Magazine*, *Lantern Review*, *Split This Rock*'s *The Quarry*, and *The Margins*. She is a fellow of the Asian American literary organization Kundiman.

"A Year of Collective Isolation" is prompted by Seema Reza.

**Courtney LeBlanc** is the author of the full length collections *Exquisite Bloody, Beating Heart* (Riot in Your Throat) and *Beautiful & Full of Monsters* (Vegetarian Alcoholic Press). She is also the founder and Editor-in-Chief of Riot in Your Throat, an independent poetry press. Follow her on twitter: @wordperv, and IG: @wordperv79

"Praise the Dark" is after Joy Harjo's "Praise the Rain," prompted by Joy Jacobson on September 9, 2020. The poem is originally published in *Janus Literary*, reprinted here by permission of the author.

**Kate Lewis** is a Boston-based writer. Kate earned her B.A. in English from Boston College in 2015 and has continued her writing studies at GrubStreet, Juniper Summer Writing Institute, and the Provincetown Fine Arts Work Center. Find her on social media at @kate_the_gr9.

"Becoming" is after Ellen Bass's "What Did I Love," prompted by Seema Reza on June 18, 2020.

**Jennifer A. Minotti** is a Writer-in-Residence at the Center for Women's Health and Human

Rights at Suffolk University in Boston, MA and the founder of the *Journal of Expressive Writing*. She holds degrees from Boston University (B.S.) and Columbia University (M.A., M.Ed). Jennifer lives with her family in Cambridge, MA.

"Go, You are Not Welcomed" is after Ross Gay's "Ode to the Puritan in Me," prompted by Yesenia Montilla on September 23, 2020.

**Faisal Mohyuddin** is a writer, artist, and educator. He is the author of *The Displaced Children of Displaced Children* (Eyewear Publishing, 2018), which won the 2017 Sexton Prize in Poetry, and was selected as a 2018 Summer Recommendation of the Poetry Book Society. His work has received *Prairie Schooner*'s Edward Stanley Award, a Gwendolyn Brooks Poetry Prize from the Illinois State Library, and an Illinois Arts Council Literary Award. His recent work appears in *Poetry Magazine, Kweli, The Margins, Pleiades, The Forward Book of Poetry 2019, Chicago Quarterly Review*, and *RHINO*.

"Because Seeking Can Help a Person Be Found, And Because First They Must Learn How to Seek" is for Seema Reza and the CBAW Community, drafted during the Acrostic Workshop Faisal hosted on April 22, 2020. "Ghazal for the Diaspora" is originally published in *The Riddle of Longing* (Backbone Press), copyright © 2017 by Faisal Mohyuddin, and also appears in *The Displaced Children of Displaced Children* (Eyewear Publishing, 2018), retrieved from *Papercuts Magazine* and reprinted here by permission of the author.

**Yesenia Montilla** is an Afro-Latina poet & a daughter of immigrants. Her poetry has appeared in *Gulf Coast, Prairie Schooner*, Academy of American Poets *Poem-a-Day* & others. She received her MFA from Drew University in poetry & poetry in translation. She is a CantoMundo graduate fellow & NYFA 2020 fellow. Her first collection *The Pink Box* was Longlisted for a PEN award in 2016. Her second collection *Muse Found in a Colonized Body* is forthcoming (Four Way Books, 2022).

"a brief meditation on breath" is originally published in Poem-a-Day on July 21, 2020 by the Academy of American Poets, copyright © 2020 by Yesenia Montilla, reprinted here by permission of the author.

**Diane Neff** is a former training manager, professor, college dean, and US Navy officer. Her poetry has appeared in the anthologies *Encore* (National Federation of State Poetry Societies), *Cadence* (Florida State Poets Association), and *Revelry* (The Gwendolyn Brooks Writers Association of Florida). She is employed by Seminole County Public Libraries.

"Time" is after Stephen Dunn's "Circular," prompted by Seema Reza on January 15, 2021.

**Cynthia Dewi Oka** is the author of *Fire Is Not a Country* (2021) and *Salvage* (2017) from Northwestern University Press, and *Nomad of Salt and Hard Water* (2016) from Thread Makes Blanket Press. A recipient of the Tupelo Quarterly Poetry Prize and the Leeway Transformation Award, her writing has appeared in *The Atlantic, POETRY*, Academy of American Poets' *Poem-a-Day, The Rumpus, PANK, Guernica, ESPNW*, and elsewhere. In collaboration with Philadelphia Contemporary, Friends of the Rail Park, and Asian Arts Initiative, her experimental poem, "Future Revisions," was exhibited at the Rail Park billboard in Philadelphia from July to August 2021. She has taught creative writing at Bryn Mawr College and is a 2021-2022 Poet in Residence at the Amy Clampitt House in Lenox,

MA. She is originally from Bali, Indonesia.

"Pastoral in Which a Deer's Thirst is the Tragic Hero" is originally published in *Hypoallergenic* and forthcoming in *Fire is Not a Country*, reprinted here by permission of the author.

**Diana Osborn**, paramedic, poet, painter, potter, now nomad remembering ultramarathon running adventures, epic mountain climbs, and a cross-country bicycle voyage with babies (one in utero). She raised a quilt shop, a couple houses, two sons, three cats, many chickens, and lots of solanaceous vegetables with her husband of 34 years.

"Holding and Why" is after Megan Alpert's "What We Kept," prompted by Seema Reza on January 12, 2021.

**Jennifer Patterson** is a grief worker who uses plants, breath, and words to explore survivorhood, body(ies) and healing. A queer and trans affirming and centering, trauma-experienced herbalist and breathwork facilitator, Jennifer offers sliding scale care as a practitioner through her private practice Corpus Ritual and is a member of The Breathe Network and Breathwork for Recovery. She is the author of *The Power of Breathwork: Simple Practices to Promote Wellbeing* (Quarto). Editor of the anthology *Queering Sexual Violence: Radical Voices from Within the Anti- Violence Movement* (2016), Jennifer speaks across the country, and has had writing published in places like *VIDA: Women in Literary Arts, 580 Split, OCHO: A Journal of Queer Arts, Nat. Brut, The Establishment, HandJob*, and *The Feminist Wire*. You can find more at corpusritual.com.

"What I Know" is prompted by Seema Reza's "What do you know about magic?" prompt on February 19, 2021.

**Martha E. Pedersen** is a 14-year Navy Veteran and third-generation veteran. She loves travel, learning, National Parks, and flowing water. Her writing spans fiction, nonfiction, and memoir with a dash of poetry. A Michigan native, she lives in North Carolina with her husband and two cats.

"How to Feed the Black Bears" is prompted by Amelia Bane's "What can I take really seriously that doesn't deserve it" Comedy prompt on June 4, 2020.

**Jason Magabo Perez** is the author of *This is for the mostless*. Recent Artist-in-Residence at the Center for Art and Thought, Perez is Assistant Professor of Ethnic Studies at California State University San Marcos and the inaugural Community Arts Fellow at the Bulosan Center for Filipino Studies.

"Beneath These Hands" is after Arthur Kayzakian, with nods to the CBAW brainstorm: images and lines shared by participants on May 22, 2020, prompted by Hari Alluri.

Lieutenant Colonel **Edgar Farr Russell III**, USAF (Retired), is a fine artist, writer, director, and performer. His art was selected for the Joslyn Art Museum's Biennial XX. His plays have been produced for NPR, the stage, and television. Russell has performed at The Library of Congress and The Kennedy Center.

"Home to Me Is / Leaving Is" is after Dilruba Ahmed's "Phase One," prompted by Seema Reza on November 18, 2020.

**Carla Sameth**'s memoir, *One Day on the Gold Line*, was published by Black Rose (2019) and her chapbook, *What Is Left*, is from dancing girl press (2021). Her work appears in literary journals and anthologies. A Pasadena Rose Poet, a Pride Poet and a former PEN Teaching Artist, Carla teaches creative writing.

"[I am a woman of 62 years old]" is after Mary Oliver's "Work," prompted by Seema Reza on February 5, 2021.

**Jon Sands** is a winner of the 2018 National Poetry Series, selected for his second book, *It's Not Magic* (Beacon Press, 2019). He hosts an interview series on IG Live called Ps & Qs. You can follow him at @iAmJonSands. His work has been featured in the *New York Times*, as well as anthologized in *The Best American Poetry*. He teaches at Brooklyn College, Urban Word NYC, and for over a decade has facilitated a weekly writing workshop for adults at Baily House, an HIV/AIDS service center in East Harlem. He tours extensively as a poet, but lives in Brooklyn.

**Jackie Schaffner** lives and writes in Fontana, California. She loves to photograph horses and dreams of doing that in the wild someday. The CBAW writing workshops have been a remarkable source of inspiration and encouragement for her, and her gratitude is boundless. This is her first publication.

"Triptych" is prompted by Seema Reza on August 14, 2020, October 16, 2020, and January 15, 2021.

**Anne R. Z. Schulman** was born in a Displaced Persons Camp in Austria and immigrated to America as a young child. She has taught English and Human Rights courses for many years. Though her published works have been poetry, she has undertaken writing memoir. "I want to share the stories of my courageous family."

"All They Have" is after Ira Sukrungruang's "After the Hysterectomy," prompted Shuly Xóchitl Cawood on November 4, 2020.

**Erik Schwab** is a former English major and editor living in Seattle, Washington. He had gone 30 years without writing a poem until he found his way to CBAW, and is grateful.

"Arrival" is after Mary Oliver's "Work," prompted by Seema Reza on February 5, 2021.

**Cyrus Sepahbodi** is an Iranian-American poet and writer. He has hosted readings such as Lamplight and the Worst Poetry Reading. He has performed across the US and is a co-founder of Mad Mouth Poetry and Mad About Ink poetry organizations. He lives with Ruth and their cat Louis in Sacramento.

"To All the Men I've Loved Before" is for Arthur Kayzakian, prompted by Hari Alluri.

**Ruby Singh** was born in the Crow's Nest Pass and now calls the lands of the xʷməθkʷəy̓əm, Sḵwx̱wú7mesh, and səl̓ílwətaʔɬ/Selilwitulh Nations (Vancouver BC) home. Singh's creativity crosses the boundaries of music, poetry, visual art, photography and film. His personal and collaborative works have been presented across Turtle Island, India, Germany and the UK. www.rubysingh.ca.

"Between Ribs and Courage" is after Faisal Mohyuddin's "Ghazal for the Diaspora," prompted by Hari Alluri on August 19, 2020.

**Sage Sparrow** is passionate about the healing power of words. She is a member of the Los Angeles Poets & Writer's Collective. Her poetry has been published in *ONTHEBUS* Issue #25 WAR Inside out, and the *Side-Eye on the Apocalypse* anthology.

"Forgiveness" is after Dilruba Ahmed's "Phase One," prompted by Seema Reza on November 18, 2020.

**Aissatou Sunjata** is a retired Librarian. "Writing has been cathartic, my saving grace. Writing for many years, I met many poets admired when a young poet shaping my own words. Now, at 62 years old, "Rumination" cannot be any more Testimony of my Truth and Elegy of my life lived so far.

"Rumination" is after Matthew Olzmann's "Build, Now, a Monument," prompted by Seema Reza on February 19, 2021.

**Jim Tritten** is a retired Navy carrier pilot who lives in a semi-rural village in New Mexico with his Danish author/artist wife and four cats.

"I Am From" is after George Ella Lyon's "Where I'm From," prompted by Seema Reza.

**Shana Turner**'s writing includes threads of front porches, racial tensions, stretch marks, kitchen tables, coming of age, queerness, lives interrupted by violence, natural human magic and intricacies of working-class culture. She is currently editing her first novel, *We Are Not Angels*.

"A Poem for Bill Withers [a record of April 4, 2020]" is prompted by Seema Reza.

**Laura Van Prooyen** is author of three collections of poetry: *Frances of the Wider Field* (forthcoming from Lily Poetry Review Books, 2021) *Our House Was on Fire* (Ashland Poetry Press), nominated by Philip Levine and winner of the McGovern Prize, and *Inkblot and Altar* (Pecan Grove Press). She is also co-author with Gretchen Bernabei of *Text Structures from Poetry*, a book of writing lessons for educators of grades 4-12 (Corwin Literacy). www.lauravanprooyen.com

"Dark Praise" is first published in *Spoon River Poetry Review* and will appear in *Frances of the Wider Field*, reprinted here by permission of the author.

**Ben Weakley** spent fourteen years in the U.S. Army. His poetry appears in the anthology, *Our Best War Stories*, by Middle West Press, as well as various other publications. He won first place in the Heroes' Voices National Poetry Contest, 2019. He lives in Northeast Tennessee with his family and a red-tick hound named Camo.

"Thirteen Times I Know You Can Hear Me" is after Wallace Stevens' "Thirteen Ways of Looking at a Blackbird" and Adrienne Rich's "Dedications," prompted by Seema Reza.

**Kendra Whitfield** writes and lives at the southern edge of the Northern Boreal Forest. She can often be found napping in sunbeams, enjoying cocktails on the porch, and watching backyard wildlife.

"Physick" is after Ellen Bass's "Eating the Bones," prompted by Seema Reza on November 20, 2020.

**Miden Wood** is a writer and illustrator from Virginia. She has been taking workshops with CBAW since April of 2020, and is grateful for the community she found there, and for all the work she has gotten to witness this past year. More of her work can be found at www.instagram.com/midenw.

"Advice for Those Whose Moth Got Out" is after Nazim Hikmet's "Some Advice to Those Who Will Serve Time in Prison" & Claudia Rankine's "Routine for an Insomniac," prompted by Jon Sands on June 24, 2020.

**Seema Yasmin** is an Emmy Award-winning journalist, medical doctor, and author. A fiction fellow of the Kundiman and Tin House workshops, she is the author of four books including *Muslim Women Are Everything*, *Viral BS: Medical Myths and Why We Fall for Them*, and *If God is a Virus*, poems based on her reporting on the Ebola epidemic in West Africa. Yasmin is a medical analyst for CNN and a correspondent for Conde Nast Entertainment. Her writing appears in *Rolling Stone*, *The New York Times*, *WIRED*, *Scientific American*, and other outlets.

"Disease Is Not the Only Thing That Spreads" is originally published in *If God Is a Virus*, copyright © 2021 by Seema Yasmin, retrieved from The Pulitzer Center, reprinted here by permission of the author and Haymarket Books.

**cd ybarra** was born in San Diego, but calls Nebraska home. Coming from an exclusively Naval family, she had to be different and raised a middle finger to tradition by joining the United States Army in 1998. She is grateful for the incredible creative space provided by CBAW.

"[I am from...]" is after George Ella Lyon's "Where I'm From," prompted by Seema Reza.

# Gratitudes

Gratitude to all the facilitators and to the writers whose work inspired not only the pieces included here, but so much crucial writing since the inception of Community Building Art Works. Breakthroughs have come because of you, and transformations: many.

To the participants in CBAW Workshops since the beginning, you are why. To the participants in the virtual workshops—from March, 2020 to February, 2021—in which the pieces gathered here were first drafted: may this work honor the ongoing work you've done before and since, the ongoing work you do: so much.

To the Readers: you made this book. And on its journey, you made joyful moments abound: this is yours.

Joe Merritt: the cover, its wings: thank you.

Institutional gratitudes.

Readers' gratitudes.

Seema's personal gratitudes.

*—Fin—*

CPSIA information can be obtained
at www.ICGtesting.com
Printed in the USA
BVHW030724031221
622949BV00003B/23

9 780578 301556